The Philippines
Nation of Islands

by ALDEN CUTSHALL
Professor of Geography
University of Illinois (Chicago)

A SEARCHLIGHT ORIGINAL
under the general editorship of

GEORGE W. HOFFMAN
University of Texas

G. ETZEL PEARCY
United States
Department of State

D. VAN NOSTRAND COMPANY, INC.
PRINCETON, NEW JERSEY

TORONTO

LONDON

NEW YORK

D. VAN NOSTRAND COMPANY, INC.
120 Alexander St., Princeton, New Jersey
(*Principal Office*)
24 West 40 Street, New York 18, New York

D. VAN NOSTRAND COMPANY, LTD.
358, Kensington High Street, London, W.14, England

D. VAN NOSTRAND COMPANY (Canada), LTD.
25 Hollinger Road, Toronto 16, Canada

———————

COPYRIGHT © 1964, BY
D. VAN NOSTRAND COMPANY, INC.

———————

Published simultaneously in Canada by
D. VAN NOSTRAND COMPANY (Canada), LTD.

———————

———————

PRINTED IN THE UNITED STATES OF AMERICA

Preface

On occasion, the Republic of the Philippines has been described as a showcase of democracy in Asia or a testing ground for Western ideas in an Oriental setting. It is more than that. For eastern and southern Asia, the Republic demonstrates a renaissance in economic growth and technical progress. Amid tropical forests, volcanic peaks, and Spanish cathedrals, and despite disruptive forces of varying magnitude, the Filipinos are forging a new nation.

The approach to a study of an area cannot be other than geographic. This book attempts to emphasize the physical-cultural-political relationships of the new nation. Man and his natural environment are inseparable. Life patterns in the Philippines reflect the noncontiguous character of an insular state. Yet history records the evolution of a fairly compact unit, to some extent like Britain and Japan. Contact between the islands has been rather easy, but intercourse over land routes remained a difficult problem until quite recently. The basic agricultural economy reflects facts of mountains and moisture, for seasonality of precipitation is oftentimes as important as the amount of rainfall received.

For some underdeveloped countries, development plans are still only paper dreams and little progress has been made in implementing them, possibly because of unsettled internal conditions as in Vietnam and Indonesia. In contrast, the Philippines has made considerable progress, despite programing difficulties, shortages of qualified senior personnel in critical areas, and similar problems. Lack of sufficient capital to finance investment has been a major handicap to sustained economic progress. There have been charges of fiscal irresponsibility and at times evidence of political instability. Both have been largely overcome. The country has shown reasonable progress and has assumed regional leadership in that large Southeast Asian power vacuum that lies perilously close to the Communist bloc and has become a primary target of Communist expansionist ambitions.

3

This book is written for the purpose of making the Philippines more understandable to Americans. Most of the book is meant to be an introduction, but a reasonably intimate introduction, to the 30,000,000 Filipinos whose nation is an American ally in the complex bipolar world of today.

If the author were to list all those to whom he is indebted for an appreciation and understanding of the Philippines, it would take several pages. The University of Illinois deserves thanks for two sabbatical leaves which made possible study and travel in the Philippines, and for a subsequent appointment to the University's Center for Advanced Study for research and writing that included the preparation of this manuscript. Gratitude is expressed to the United States Educational Foundation in the Philippines for generous grants to travel, study, and teach in the Philippines. The author wishes to express thanks to the many Filipinos—travel companions, students, short-time neighbors, and unnamed officials—who with their warm hospitality and quiet courtesy made it a joy to gather and assemble information about their country; and special thanks to Dominador Z. Rosell, currently President of the Philippine Geographical Society, for innumerable personal and professional courtesies over the past several years. Particular thanks are due to G. Etzel Pearcy for general encouragement and specific comments as this manuscript was being prepared. It is a pleasure to dedicate this monograph to my wife, Freda, who has struggled with my Philippine materials for years, and to Arlene and Alden Jr., who on occasion have presented a point of view from a different perspective.

ALDEN CUTSHALL

Lombard, Illinois

Contents

PREFACE   3

1 SOUTHEAST ASIAN SETTING   7

2 COLONY, COMMONWEALTH, AND NATION   11
Spanish Philippines, 11; The American Period, 13; Commonwealth Transition, 15; Japanese Interlude, 18; The New Nation, 19

3 PEOPLE, RACES, AND MODES OF LIVING   24
Racial Factors, 24; Life in the Philippines, 26; Population and Demographic Behavior, 32

4 LANGUAGES, RELIGION, AND EDUCATION   37
Linguistic Diversity, 37; The Role of Religion, 39; Philippine Education, 42

5 PRODUCTION, PATTERNS, AND PROBLEMS OF AGRICULTURE   46
Food Crops and Subsistence Agriculture, 48; Commercial Agriculture, 52; The Animal Industry, 58; An Evaluation, 59

6 MINERAL RESOURCES   61
Precious Metals, 61; Base Metals and Ferro-Alloys, 62; Energy Resources, 64; Non-Metallic Minerals, 66; The Mineral Endowment, 66

7 EMERGING INDUSTRIAL PATTERNS   68
Pattern of Manufacturing, 1945-1950, 69; Industrial Growth Since 1950, 70; Dominance of the Manila Industrial District, 73; Impetus to Manufacturing, 75; Handicaps to Industrialization, 76; The Outlook for Industrialization, 77

8 PHILIPPINE COMMERCIAL CENTERS, TRANSPORTATION, AND COMMERCE   80
The Philippine Core Area, 80; Regional Centers, 81; Transportation, 83

9 CHARACTER OF NATION   93
Philippine Nationalism, 93; Governmental Operation, 96; Law and Order, 98; Politics and Leadership, 100

10 FOREIGN POLICY AND FOREIGN TRADE   105
      Philippine Role in the United Nations, 105; Nation-to-Nation
      Relations, 107; Status of National Boundaries, 117; Foreign
      Trade, 119
11 THE PHILIPPINES AND THE UNITED STATES   122
      Military Ties and Strategic Relationships, 123; Economic
      Relationships, 124; Political and Social Associations, 126
    BIBLIOGRAPHY   129
    INDEX   130

Maps

1 THE PHILIPPINES IN ITS SOUTHEAST ASIAN SETTING   9
2 THE PHILIPPINES   16
3 PHILIPPINE COMMERCIAL PRODUCTION   51
4 PHILIPPINE TRANSPORTATION   91

1   *Southeast Asian Setting*

THE Philippines is a young, democratic nation on the margin of turbulent, tropical East Asia. It represents somewhat of an experiment or a proving ground for Western political, economic, and social institutions in an Oriental setting. The Republic has been described as a transition zone between East and West in the Pacific. Geographically, the country lies within the realm of Southeast Asia.

The physical geography of Southeast Asia remains unchanged, the economy is in slow transition, the politics is turbulent. The nine countries[1] that make up this region are emerging, viable nations. Each country has a strong spirit of nationalism, that indescribable group feeling or national psychology that gives the people a sense of belonging together, but a regional politics is yet to develop. The realm as a whole is characterized by an incomplete development of crop land. There are sparsely settled regions and overpopulated areas. Southeast Asia is best characterized as a geographical realm that is diverse or complex in geomorphology, climatic conditions, mineral wealth, agricultural development and products, ethnic and linguistic components, political heritage, and potential economy. The Philippines, the first of the countries of Southeast Asia to achieve independence after World War II, is a part of this complex land and economy, and illustrates the regional complexity many times within its national domain.

Southeast Asia is a vast area of both land and water. (See Figure 1.) Manila is 1,500 miles from Singapore, approximately the distance from the Canadian border to the Gulf of Mexico and almost as far as from London to Istanbul. Surface transportation is slow. The rise of air transport has given a new importance to the area. Bangkok and Rangoon are off the principal arteries of sea travel,

[1] Burma, Thailand, Laos, Cambodia, North and South Vietnam, Indonesia, Malaysia and the Philippines.

yet along with Manila and Singapore, both have become major centers of international air travel.

Within insular Southeast Asia the Republic of the Philippines consists of more than 7,000 islands, about 800 of them inhabited, that extend through 16 degrees of latitude (about 1,100 miles). (See Figure 2, pp. 16-17.) Luzon, the largest island, is comparable in size to Guatemala, Bulgaria, or the state of Ohio. The total land area of the Philippines, approximately twice that of Illinois, is equal to 10 Switzerlands.

Southeast Asia is peopled principally by Malays, and the numerous indigenous languages and dialects are Malayan in character. However, the Philippine dialects contain many Spanish words, largely nouns for which no Tagalog, Visayan, or Ilokano word exists. English is the second language and the language of instruction in the Philippines, something quite different than in Indonesia or Vietnam. Chinese comprise the principal minority group in every country of Southeast Asia, and Chinese is spoken by most of the residents of the Chinese communities.

In religion too the Philippines shows a marked difference from its neighbors. Mainland Southeast Asia, except Malaya, is Buddhist. Indonesia and Malaysia are predominantly Moslem. In contrast, the Philippines is primarily Christian, the only Christian country in all of Asia. The Filipinos are very proud of this fact. They pride themselves too, for being the third largest English-speaking country in terms of population.[2] These elements have contributed to Philippine nationalism, and they are elements that help to set the Filipino apart from other Southeast Asian residents to whom he is racially akin.

The Philippines is an insular arc, largely of volcanic origin and on occasion endangered by typhoons. The intervening seas and the rugged, oftentimes inaccessible interior uplands have tended to isolate various groups from one another. As a result, local dialects and customs have evolved. The community, not the nation, is supreme in many matters. In the Philippines, as in Indonesia, Japan, and

---

[2] This statement assumes that all or most Filipinos speak English, thus ranking the Philippines behind the United States and the United Kingdom, but ahead of Canada.

ancient Greece, the sea was the means of communication and trade throughout early history. It has been the unifying element or agent, as areas or settlements frequently are separated from one another by rugged uplands of dense, impenetrable vegetation.

FIGURE 1

THE PHILIPPINES IN ITS SOUTHEAST ASIAN SETTING

In any final analysis the basic tensions of the Philippines are economic, rather than sectional, religious, or political. The three broad divisions of the country (Luzon, the Visayas, and Mindanao) do not represent the type of regionalism that might lead to great sectional conflict and disintegration of the Republic. There is a Moro problem that has not been completely solved, but there is no possibility of a Philippine Pakistan. National unity has been less of a problem than internal security. Because democratic processes take a local flavor, there may be political terrorism and election-eve murders. But in national politics the major parties have been similar in outlook. The Filipino can count on the resident of Malacañan, the Philippine White House, to keep his country firmly aligned with the West on major issues.

However, cleavage along economic lines has been serious. It has permitted agrarian unrest in parts of the country, contributed to the difficulties associated with import controls, and limited the growth of manufacturing in some areas of production. One further disadvantage of Philippine economic progress may be an over-optimism on the part of the planners. Often there has been an attempt to do too much, too soon, with too little. Philippine technology and skills have not kept pace with the changing economic advances. Vested interests have retarded, in some cases seriously handicapped, a normal, well-rounded development of the domestic economy.

Like other new nations of Southeast Asia, the Philippine nation-state is primarily a colonial legacy and is based upon the political unification of diverse culture groups. The colonial period was characterized by a minimum of political, economic, and geographical integration. No local language is the mother tongue of more than 25 percent of the Philippine population. So, for the foreseeable future, the Philippine economy is confronted with extreme language diversity at the local level, which complicates communication, handicaps economic activity, and hampers political unity. National unity is diluted to a greater extent by cultural and social differences than by geographical fragmentation.

2 *Colony, Commonwealth, and Nation*

T HE Philippines is the only nation in Southeast Asia that was subjected to Western colonization before it had developed a centralized governmental structure. Although the islands were undoubtedly known to Chinese traders by the tenth century A.D. and both Hindu and Moslem contacts preceded the arrival of the first Europeans, the Spanish explorers found no recognizable political organization of any magnitude. There was no élite culture, no royal court, no military subjugation, hence no group that ruled over a large territory or over thousands of people. In fact, the largest effective political unit was the *barangay,* a kinship group at the village level. A union or confederation of barangays frequently developed, but seldom endured.

SPANISH PHILIPPINES

Discovered by Magellan in 1521, the Philippines were claimed for Spain and named for Prince Philip, later Philip II. Subsequent expeditions left no permanent imprint until Miguel Lopez de Legaspi was appointed governor and established a settlement on Cebu in May, 1565. Most of his forces were transferred to Panay in 1569, and Manila, then a bamboo-barricaded village, became the administrative center of the archipelago in 1671. From this humble beginning Manila has developed into the most Westernized city in Monsoon Asia. The conquest of Luzon proceeded rapidly, and by 1700 Spanish authority had been extended over most of the coastal and lowland areas north of Mindanao. The Moros of the southern islands and the Igorots in the mountains of northern Luzon continued effective local resistance throughout the Spanish regime.

Spanish colonial motives were primarily commercial and secondarily religious. The former, as elsewhere during this period, was geared to exploitation rather than permanent economic development. Tribute was levied upon the Filipinos immediately upon conquest. This over-all policy with its semi-feudal agrarian system of tax farming (the *encomienda*), together with the harsh attitude of the Spanish administrators, contributed materially to the insurrectionist movement in the latter years of the nineteenth century. Magellan's attempt to Catholicize the natives of spiceless Cebu ended in failure and ultimately in his death. But in most cases, friars marched with soldiers, and conversion to Catholicism was generally peaceful and, with qualifications, successful, except in those areas never completely subdued by the Spaniards. The union of church and state was effective and realistic; the Governor-General was also civil head of the church throughout the period of Spanish rule. As an indirect result of, or a corollary to Spanish rule, the Spanish language was superimposed upon the basic Malayan society. Furthermore, there developed a large group of *mestizos* (people of mixed blood), part Spanish and part Malay, a result of generations in which there were no Spanish women in the Philippines.

The Spanish did practically nothing to advance the people politically or otherwise train them for self government. Within the Spanish central government in Manila, Filipinos held no responsible positions. Several provinces remained under military rule until the end of the Spanish regime; in those areas there was virtually no native participation in government. Filipino leadership was possible only in pacified areas and only below the provincial level. The barangay was modified to become a territorial unit, a part of the *municipia,* which was a subdivision of a province somewhat intermediate between a U. S. county and a political township. Actually the barangay lost almost all governmental significance. The position of the *datu,* or headman, originally hereditary, was made appointive and consisted primarily of collecting taxes. The power of the church became dominant as the parish priest was oftentimes the only Spaniard in town and a member of most of the administrative boards and commissions that had final say in municipal decision-making. The Philippines were represented in the Spanish Parliament only from 1810 to 1837, and then only irregularly.

The seeds of the Philippine revolt against Spain were planted indiscriminantly during three centuries of harsh Spanish rule. But a successful revolution requires educated leadership. Initially the seeds sprouted and died because this leadership was lacking, for the tenant farmer in 1800 had no access to education. By the end of the nineteenth century a rapidly increasing number of young men were being educated in Manila, and a lesser number had found it possible to afford a European education. Once exposed to European nationalism, they shouted for Philippine independence. A revolt against Spanish rule in 1896 was put down. It later broke out anew, and by the time the United States acquired the islands from Spain in February, 1899, it had made considerable progress. It was not until April, 1901, that General Emilio Aguinaldo, the leader of the revolt, surrendered to U.S. authorities.

THE AMERICAN PERIOD

After the Spanish-American War the Filipinos realized that they had merely changed masters. But it quickly became clear that the change was for the better. The new colonial power was one that had experienced colonial rule and that had thrown off the yoke of its former ruler by revolution. It was, therefore, highly sympathetic to Filipino national aspirations, and gave practical expression to this sympathy in the solemn commitment to grant independence to the Philippines "as soon as a stable government shall be established therein."

From the beginning United States policy stressed a progressively increasing amount of self government. After internal unity was established, autonomous powers were delegated to Filipinos as qualified leaders demonstrated their ability to handle domestic affairs.

Education and public health were the foundation of Philippine development. American schools were opened and American teachers supplied as rapidly as appropriations permitted. In the absence of a common language, English became the medium of instruction and American textbooks were used. The early American teachers were gradually replaced by Filipinos, most of them graduates of insular English-language schools and Filipino colleges. Except in private schools, education was free, non-religious, and generally coeducational. However, most pupils left school at the end of the third grade.

From American acquisition of the Philippines in 1898 to the proclamation of the Republic in 1946, a complex progression from outright American military government to complete Filipinization of the administration unfolded. The development was sporadic. It evolved unevenly with recurrent retrogressions interspersed along the trail of progression, a reflection of the conflicting Philippine policy in the United States and the shifting legislative majorities. It was not that America lacked a Philippine policy, as often has been stated. In reality, two conflicting lines of policy vied for support in America's relations with the Philippines from the very beginning. The first emphasized dependence of the Islands on the United States within the framework of an American colonial empire. The other fostered Philippine independence from the very inception of American relations with the Islands. The apparent contradictions in the Philippine policy of the United States reflected the shifting balance of power between these two diametrically opposed trends of American thought. Sometimes one, sometimes the other assumed the upper hand. On occasion both were rather evenly balanced in a single legislative act.

In essence, the conflict reflected America's growing pains as a world power. The Jeffersonian and Lincolnian concepts of democracy and national freedom that epitomized America's emergence from colonial status to independent nationhood and the development of America's own potentialities and resources were challenged by new political doctrines reflecting America's economic expansion and entrance into world markets. In the well-chosen words of A. Whitney Griswold:

> Amid the clash of arms the Philippine Archipelago became an American colony. These Islands, lying some six hundred miles off the Chinese coast, bear no conceivable relation to American supremacy in the Caribbean, much less to the continental security of the United States. With their annexation the United States emerged from its habitual, self-sufficient abode in the Western Hemisphere and entered the limitless realm of world politics, naval rivalry and imperial

dominion. A step so unprecedented could not have failed to influence the character of American diplomacy in every quarter of the globe, and nowhere more profoundly than in that which included the Philippines.[1]

COMMONWEALTH TRANSITION

With the establishment of the Philippine Commonwealth in 1935 —a result of the Tydings-McDuffie Act, or Philippine Independence Act, passed in 1934—the colony became essentially a self-governing state except for external affairs and some aspects of law and order.[2] The Commonwealth was set up after the adoption of a constitution and was administered by an elected Filipino executive, Manuel Quezon. The Tydings-McDuffie Act specifically provided for complete independence after a 10-year interim period of Commonwealth status and thereby provided for a reasonable period of politico-economic transition.

In retrospect, the Commonwealth proved itself a workable transitional form of government. It satisfied most of the aspirations of the Filipino people as well as their leaders. The operation of the powers reserved to the United States was not conspicuous. The weaknesses were economic rather than political, hence not a fault of Commonwealth organization *per se*. As a result of a realization of tenant farmers that their low economic status might be altered through organized, militant action, a rising demand for agrarian reform developed. Although not ignored, the movement was underestimated, and thereby the seeds of the postwar Hukbalahap uprising were firmly planted. Secondly, there was little constructive

[1] A. Whitney Griswold, *The Far Eastern Policy of the United States,* Harcourt Brace and Company, New York, 1938, pp. 3-4.

[2] Supervision of foreign affairs remained with the United States and the U. S. Congress maintained control over the size and structure of the Philippine national debt. Approval of the U. S. President was required for all laws concerned with currency, coinage, imports, exports and immigration. The United States might intervene in internal Commonwealth affairs in order to preserve the Commonwealth government, life, property and individual liberty as provided by constitution. The United States retained rights to maintain and acquire military bases in the archipelago, to quarter American forces there, and to join with these forces all military forces organized by the Philippine government.

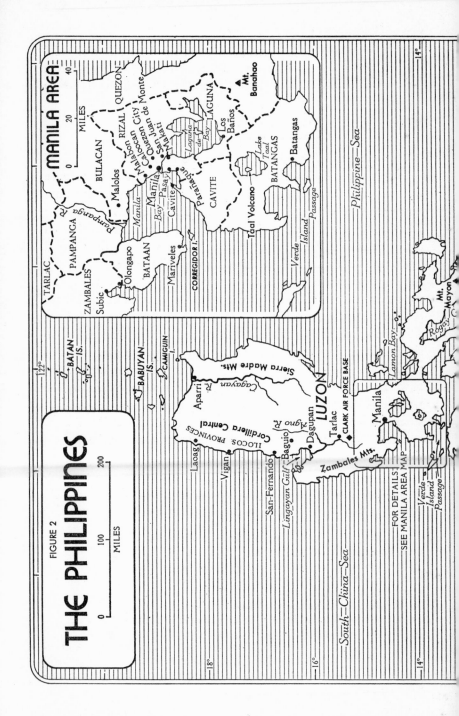

FIGURE 2

THE PHILIPPINES

MILES
0   100   200

MANILA AREA

MILES
0   20   40

TARLAC

PAMPANGA

Pampanga R.

ZAMBALES

Subic
Olongapo
BATAAN
Mariveles
CORREGIDOR I.

BULACAN

Malolos

Malabon
Caloocan City
Manila
Pasay
Cavite
Parañaque
Pasig
Bay

CAVITE

Taal Volcano

Lake Taal

BATANGAS

Batangas

RIZAL QUEZON

Quezon City
San Juan de Monte
Makati

LAGUNA

Laguna de Bay

Los Baños

▲ Mt.
Banahao

Verde — Island — Passage

Philippine — Sea

122°

BATAN
IS.

BABUYAN
IS.

CAMIGUIN

Aparri

Cagayan R.

Sierra Madre Mts.

ILOCOS PROVINCES

Laoag

Vigan

San Fernando

Lingayan Gulf

Baguio

Cordillera Central

Dagupan

Agno R.

LUZON

Tarlac

CLARK AIR FORCE BASE

Zambales Mts.

Manila

Lamon Bay

Mt.
Mayon

Rogay

South — China — Sea

FOR DETAILS
SEE MANILA AREA MAP

Verde —
Island —
Passage

18°

16°

14°

14°

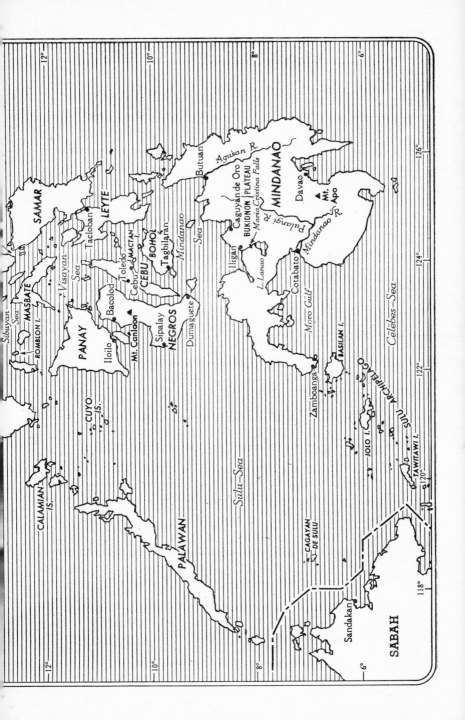

leadership in the area of economic preparation for independence. It was assumed, often desired, that the Philippines retain its dominant agricultural economy. Therefore, there was no realistic attempt to expand the minor manufacturing activities then present and thereby permit the new nation a slightly more diversified base from which to begin its independent operations.[3]

JAPANESE INTERLUDE

Japanese forces attacked the Philippines on December 8 (on the Asian side of the International Date Line), 1941, and effective U. S. striking power was neutralized in rapid order. Manila was soon declared an open city (January 2, 1942), and American and Filipino defenders retired to Bataan and Corregidor, where they held out until May 6, 1942. President Manuel Quezon, Vice President Sergio Osmeña, and other governmental leaders were evacuated by submarine before surrender and set up a government-in-exile in Washington, D. C.

Because of the advanced stage of the Philippine preparation for independence, the Japanese tried to conceal their mailed fist with a velvet glove. Their policies differed from those used elsewhere in Southeast Asia. Independence was promised; a constitution was drafted, although it was never submitted to the people; a puppet "republic" was inaugurated in October of 1943 with José Laurel as "president." Some of the Filipino leaders apparently were willing followers of Japanese propaganda of "Asia for the Asiatics" and the "Greater East Asia Co-Prosperity Sphere." Others succumbed under pressure or through fear for themselves or their families; still others did so purely for economic gain or political favors.

For most of the Filipinos, the three and one-half years of occupation were years of real hardship. The Japanese economic program led to poverty, discontent, and disaster. The social program was negative and ineffective. Whatever communications, industries, and mines remained in operation were run by the Japanese military. Interisland shipping was appropriated for military purposes. Un-

[3] For a most complete, authoritative study of the Commonwealth government see Joseph R. Hayden, *The Philippines: A Study in National Development,* Macmillan, 1942.

employment increased, salaries and wages were reduced, and the cost of living increased, largely because of a scarcity of goods. Hoarding was commonplace and a black market in rice flourished. The Japanese occupation currency, known as "Mickey Mouse" money, was worthless; barter became essential to survival, and a Manila family with farm relatives in a nearby province was viewed with envy by its neighbors. The death rate rose, largely as a result of inadequate Japanese health-control measures and an acute short-age of medicines and medical supplies. There was strict control over radio and the press. Filipinos were subjected to indignities and other maltreatment at the hands of the occupying forces.

The response was passive resistance and support of guerrilla ac-tivities. No amount of intimidation could induce the Filipinos to abandon the urge for freedom. There was never any real doubt that America would return; to this end the leaders of both countries had wholeheartedly pledged their best efforts. News was circulated by printed handbills and by word of mouth. Resentment and clandestine raids were directed toward the Japanese and toward those who collaborated with them. The Filipinos applied their indi-vidual ingenuity to harassing and killing the Japanese. Personal stories of Americans interned at Santo Tomas and elsewhere are replete with incidents of Filipino kindness and personal sacrifice. This unwaivering confidence in a former ruler merits real praise.

THE NEW NATION

Under American rule an understanding of democratic institutions evolved and the Filipinos developed a capacity to operate these in-stitutions for themselves. Sergio Osmeña, especially, developed a Filipino parlimentary tradition and Manuel Quezon engendered an executive tradition. Vigorously they sought independence from the United States, and there was never any doubt in their minds as to the kind of independent state that they desired. Representative gov-ernment, separation of powers, a civil-service system based on merit, and a system of public education were the cornerstones of the pro-posed Philippine political system.

It is unfortunate that the date of Philippine independence (July 4, 1946) came so shortly after the conclusion of military hostilities and amidst the destruction associated with liberation from the Japanese. Physical reconstruction and human rehabilitation competed with and did not permit proper emphasis upon the new political organization and the orderly economic development of the new nation. Of the two architects of independence, Manuel Quezon had died in exile (August, 1944) and Sergio Osmeña was an elderly and defeated leader, having lost the presidential election to Manuel Roxas (April 23, 1946) while many parts of the country were still under military control. Both Roxas and Vice-President Elpidio Quirino had been apt pupils of Quezon and Osmeña. Nonetheless, political leadership was intrusted, of necessity, to men of unproven administrative abilities at the national level and often to men further handicapped by the charge of Japanese collaboration. Under this set of circumstances, it is not surprising that internal chaos developed during the early years of the new Republic. The progress that has been made is a demonstration to the world and to the Filipinos that the Islanders had the courage and the competence to survive under the most adverse conditions.

The new Republic is organized as a political democracy with a liberal constitution patterned after the constitution of the United States. There is no legally privileged class, but in practice the government was dominated initially by a group of wealthy landowners. (This initial control of the landed aristocracy has been lessened significantly, particularly under the administration of Ramon Magsaysay, 1953-1957.)

The United States has provided great assistance to the Philippines. As independence approached it was readily apparent that there must be outside aid, both financial and technical in character, in the reconstruction and rehabilitation of the war-torn economy, to reestablish a reasonable educational system and to maintain law and order amidst the physical destruction and mass unemployment that existed immediately after liberation. U. S. legislation on these subjects included the Philippine Rehabilitation Act (Tydings Bill), the Philippine Trade Act (Bell Bill), the Philippine Military Assistance Act, and the Filipino Naturalization Act, the latter simply an amendment to the Nationality Act of 1940, which makes Filipinos racially eligible for naturalization.

The Philippine Rehabilitation Act (Public Law 370), signed by President Truman on April 30, 1946, provided a threefold type of assistance. It stipulated that Philippine war-damage claimants be granted $400 million for property destroyed or damaged as a result of actual warfare. Recipients included the highway department, railroads, shipping interests, sugar mills and other factories, schools, and universities. Farmers were reimbursed for coconut trees destroyed or carabao killed at the Leyte beachhead and other landings, if loss could be properly established. Secondly, the Commonwealth government and subsequent Republic were allocated, without reimbursement, $100 million worth of surplus property, such as military vehicles, small naval vessels and landing craft, surplus planes from the U.S. Air Force, earth-moving equipment that had been used in air field construction, clothing, and medical supplies. Finally, the Act authorized that $120 million be spent in various rehabilitation and training projects or programs. It was specifically designed to provide trained technical experts for key industries or services. Fishing trainees and future foreign-service personnel were among those sent to this country for education or other training.

The companion Philippine Trade Act (Public Law 371) provided for a continuance of free trade between the Philippines and the United States for eight years. After 1954 a gradual imposition of United States tariff duties was to be placed in effect (at the rate of five percent per year) for a period of 20 years; thereafter, beginning in 1974, full duties were to be assessed. In addition, absolute quotas were set upon exports to America of sugar, Manila hemp, rice,[4] cigars, scrap and filler tobacco, coconut oil, and pearl buttons.

As a result of complaints and criticisms by Philippine producers, processors, and exporters, and after much discussion, the 1946 trade act was amended and modified by the Laurel-Langley Agreement of December, 1954. Among about a dozen major economic stipulations, the one of greatest importance was the provision which delayed the imposition of United States duties on Philippine goods until 1959, allowing an extra five years for the Philippine economy to make a more realistic adjustment to an overseas market of Philippine export products.

[4] The Philippines have never been a rice exporter.

The Philippine Military Assistance Agreement (March 20, 1947) provided funds, material, and guidance by American personnel (Joint United States Military Advisory Group, or JUSMAG) for the training and development of Philippine military forces. The initial $20 million allotment was augmented by an additional $47 million as a result of the Magsaysay mission in 1950. The additional funds were justified on the basis of the then serious Hukbalahap dissident activities and the associated fact that responsibility for internal security was assigned to the army, a better-trained and better-disciplined agency than the Philippine constabulary.

Often associated with the Military Assistance Act, but actually a separate agreement, was the now-famous "Bases Agreement." It provided that certain American military bases would be made available on request to the Security Council of the United Nations, and that the United States would be permitted to use specifically designated naval installations in the Philippines. These initial provisions for foreign forces on Philippine soil proved to be a source of irritation to the Philippine citizenry, more political than realistic, however. Of the 11 Army bases retained in 1947, only Clark Air Force Base on Luzon has actually been utilized by American forces. And of the four naval operating areas specifically mentioned in the agreement, only Subic Bay and Sangley Point (Cavite) remain as U. S. naval bases. The bases agreement was modified in 1959, and some of its more undesirable and distasteful aspects, from a Philippine point of view, were removed.

The Philippine nation has experienced a variety of problems and pains associated with independence and growth. Some of them are a result of insularity and fragmentation; because the Philippines sprawl over considerable distances, a concentration of interests is difficult to achieve. Luzon has inherited agrarian problems from the Spanish form of land use, which no longer suits the dense population of today. The Muslim minority in the South and the influential Chinese minority within the commercial community have made unity more difficult. Relations with Japan have been uneasy, and Japanese manufactures are seen as a threat to Philippine industralization. Boundary claims on North Borneo make news, but may be more academic than realistic.

The Republic has shown continued progress, but at an irregular rate of growth, one that might best be characterized as "steady by jerks." To some extent this rate of growth and increased stability reflects the quality, energy, and thinking of the changing political leadership. President Roxas may have been a brilliant man, but the initial stigma of collaboration, postwar agrarian unrest, financial problems of the new nation, election terrors and mass frauds, the physical magnitude of reconstruction and rehabilitation, and many other frustrating elements combined to push the Philippines close to the brink of disaster during the early years of its national history. The Quirino Administration (1949-1953) showed improvement in some respects, lassitude or stagnation in other areas. The appointment of forceful, dynamic Ramon Magsaysay as Secretary of Defense (1950) was the turning point of the early years. He brought a new sense of responsibility and respectibility to the army. He broke the back of the Huk movement, destroying those he could not win over.

With Magsaysay as President (1954-1957) the Philippines reached a new plateau. He demanded an honest day's work and integrity from his appointees. He invited "bare feet to the palace," and his popularity with the masses zoomed. He may have had no foreign policy except great friendship for the United States, but he raised the Philippines to a new high of unity and morality. His death on a Cebu mountainside in March of 1957 was the tragedy of the decade. President Carlos Garcia (1957-1962) was no Ramon Maysaysay, but he was a shrewd politician. He continued many of the Magsaysay policies, but never approached the popularity of his former chief. Amid charges of corruption, nepotism, misuse of contingent funds, and unwarranted allocation of dollars, improvements were slow. But industry did expand very significantly, law and order was maintained, and the "bases issue" was resolved in an agreeable fashion. Diosdado Macapagal, elected in 1961 and installed in January of 1962, is well educated and well informed. He could become the best all-around President in the first two decades of Philippine national history.

3   *People, Races, and*
   Modes of Living

WHAT is the Filipino? The United States Supreme Court once ruled that he is not a Caucasian. The state of California has ruled that he is not a Mongolian. He has a dark skin, but historically he has been able to travel in Southern United States or study at Southern universities without "segregation incidents." He is then uniquely a Filipino, and he is known as a Filipino[1] in the world community.

The Filipino is a gregarious, congenial person and a gracious host. He loves to visit and talk with his fellow men. The weekly village market may take on a festive appearance and become as much a meeting to exchange news and views as to exchange the commodities of production. The *siesta* hour is observed, and many things are attuned to it. The Filipino loves his children and is fond of holidays, of which there are many that honor national heroes and events or patron saints of the Catholic Church. He tends to be clannish, and family ties are strong.

The Filipino really lives two lives. One involves only his family and a few close friends. It is warm, friendly, hospitable, charitable, and sincere in every respect. The other is superficial in many ways. It is the life of business and politics—and the attendant social functions. One gets to know the Filipino when he goes beneath the surface, when he knows him in his family setting.

RACIAL FACTORS

Like the United States, the Philippines has been a melting pot. The dominant racial stock is Malayan, believed to have reached the

[1] In the Philippines the term "Filipino" connotes a Christian resident of the country. Non-Christian groups are never referred to as Filipinos, but as Negritos, Igorots, Moros, Chinese, etc. They may or may not be racially akin to the Christian resident.

24

Philippines from Borneo, Sumatra, and mainland Southeast Asia. But racial mixing processes have been in operation for 4000 years; a Filipino blend has been produced. Over the centuries there has been some infusion of Indonesian and Mongoloid blood in almost every group, and some Spanish or Chinese strains appear among the leading people on all major islands of the country. Nonetheless, the racial integrity of the Malays has been maintained to a remarkable degree among lowland Filipinos, who make up more than nine-tenths of the total population.

A more detailed analysis does reveal some marked contrasts and many less obvious variations among the Philippine people. There are great differences between the Negritos, the original inhabitants who still live in the more remote uplands of some of the larger islands; the skilled Ifugao mountaineers of northern Luzon who live amid their famous rice-terraces; the sea gypsies who ply the Sulu Sea in their outrigger, canoe-type house boats; and other small groups who are different from the majority of the inhabitants and different from each other.

These relatively unassimilated pagans and the Muslim (Moro) groups form local, highly centripetal societies that are only loosely or tenuously linked with the national government and have only vague and infrequent social and cultural ties with the Christian Filipinos. In general, however, the proximity of the islands and the ease of navigation between or among them has prevented the insular isolationism that exists in some other archipelagoes. Even though nature has seldom repeated her proportions exactly in this multi-island environment, there are few racial contrasts of any great magnitude.

Despite this general apparent homogeneity, the modern Philippines continues to be characterized by cultural, linguistic, and racial complexity. Chinese, Americans, and Spaniards—in that order—constitute the largest alien minorities in the Philippines today. Pure or nearly pure Spanish strains remain in only a few areas, but Spanish *mestizos* are commonplace, the result of more than 300 years of Spanish rule. There have been thousands of American-Filipino marriages, first dating from the American occupation after the defeat of the Spanish, and this has come to include a small number of American-Moro, American-Igorot and American Negro-Christian Filipino mixtures. There are occasional Swiss, German, Norwegian, or Danish *mestizos* as well. The American community, which may number as many as 15,000 to 20,000 exclusive of government and military personnel, are prominent in mining, lumber, sugar, pineapple, abaca, and coconut interests, in export and import trade, in some of the public utilities, in petroleum processing, and in some of the other new manufacturing industries.

But the Asian racial strains dip much deeper into history. Indian and Arab Moslems reached the Philippine Archipelago about 1480. The first arrivals from mainland Southeast Asia and the Indies were primarily concerned with spreading their religion. They were followed by political chieftains, and herein lies the beginning of the modern Moros' stronghold in the Sulu Chain, Mindanao, and Palawan. Even earlier were Chinese contacts, probably dating from about 2000 B.C. Some 300,000 Chinese are interspersed throughout the islands, but are concentrated in the cities and towns. They have been the traders, shopkeepers, and money lenders throughout the Philippines for centuries. They dominate the retail trade, handle a large part of the import-export business, operate most of the rice mills, and have interests in several bus lines and some of the inter-island and coastal shipping. Undoubtedly there are several million Filipinos with lesser amounts of Chinese ancestry. Finally there is a small Indian Hindu community, about 2000 in number, largely shop owners in Manila and a few other communities. In no sense does the Indian community have the impact of the larger Chinese minority.

Hence, there are all kinds of people in the Philippines. But there are no sharp divisions of territory by races. Fundamental differences between and among the Filipinos are more religious and linguistic than racial. Divergent modes of dress and other cultural characteristics are more easily recognized than are different racial features.

LIFE IN THE PHILIPPINES

The basic philosophy of life is different from that prevailing in the United States or even in other parts of Asia. Public education is theoretically free, and certainly its cost is nominal. Public housing is in the embryonic stage. But the mine operator, *hacienda* owner, or lumber company, in part out of necessity, has adopted a parental attitude and may have provided communal housing, a clinic or dispensary, a "modern" school, or a company store, but otherwise it is "every man for himself." Cleanliness of body and clothing is ingrained, but in the countryside both the daily bath and the family laundry may be done in the nearby river or small stream or at the community well. Children, especially small boys in rural areas, run naked or wear only a shirt. Work-a-day clothes for the laboring man are the T-shirt with shorts; for rural women, a near-ankle-length wrap-around or tube skirt and a blouse.

THE RURAL COMMUNITY

The postwar Philippine barrio and oftentimes the *poblacion,* the principal community in the municipality (county), is not appreciably different from the representative prewar village and town. The community is most often built around and its life oriented to a centrally located plaza. Most plazas have a statue of José Rizal, the first Filipino to envision and fight for a government for the people. There may be a basketball court, a bandstand, a well, or community gardens. Alongside or near the plaza is the *municipio* (municipal building) and the Catholic church. These structures may have been ruined by the war. If so, they have been rebuilt or repaired. Only the school may have been moved from its former central location to a new site on the outskirts of the town where there is still room for expansion. If so, United States War Damage funds helped with its construction. The private Catholic school and convent have remained alongside the old stone church as a part of the new plaza complex. The marketplace is either alongside the plaza or at a nearby location, as are the Chinese stores. Other public facilities—the postoffice, telephone and telegraph office, electric company, and the more fully stocked stores—surround or are near the plaza. The more elaborate older residences are nearby, although newer spacious homes are less likely to have a central location. Most political, social, and religious celebrations occur in the plaza area. By definition, the plaza complex is a physical area, a segment of the town, but it is the social and cultural pivot of the community.[2] If a *poblacion* does not have a plaza, something is lacking.

Most villages and towns are crowded with houses; some of them are situated on low-lying sites that may be easily flooded. The representative town shows little evidence of planning. It developed without control and without plan, along the highway or the seashore or the mountain road. The result is a typical overcrowded settlement; and its population is still increasing, often increasing rapidly.

Coastal communities are partially, often totally, fishing settlements. The site may be a well-drained sandy shoreline, or it may be a mud flat where houses of squatters have mushroomed on the no-man's-land that is half sea and half land—a mud flat when the tide recedes, sea when the tide rises. *Bancas* (dugout canoes) lie on the beach in front of nipa-thatched homes or have been carried under the house. Out-rigger fishing boats are pushed to the edge of the sea. Fishing nets are dried on a frame of bamboo poles. In such a community people may crowd together and get into each other's way.

Farming barrios, more often on the other side of the provincial road that follows along the shoreline, are closer to the hills than are the fishing communities. These barrios are also compact and crowded, and the houses are equally small. The banca and net under or near the fisherman's house are replaced by the carabao or bullock and cart or sled. The neighborhood is friendly; the people are happy, humble, and hospitable.

Home industries in the representative town may include *sawali* and *buri* mat weaving, the making of grass brooms, or the manufacture of *bakia* (wooden slippers). If the town is a coastal community, bancas may be hewn from logs during those periods that winds make fishing unprofitable or unsafe. If it is an interior community, there may be a localized or specialized home industry, such as pottery, weaving, or woodworking.

A large community probably will have a charity clinic and a government dentist; a school nurse and doctor look after the immediate

[2] Donn V. Hart, "The Philippine Plaza Complex: A Focal Point in Cultural Change," Yale University Southeast Asia Studies, 1955, p. 1. (mimeographed).

health problems of the school children and teachers. The nearest hospital is in the provincial capital. The school has three or six grades, possibly two shifts of 40 pupils in each classroom of grades one to three, and both morning and afternoon sessions for grades four to six. The local dialect is the medium of normal communication, but English is the language of instruction in all grades above second.

There is a veneer of Christian teaching and a Western educational framework. Both have been overemphasized for the more remote segments of the country. Pre-Christian gods and godlings of the pagan Philippines still haunt and terrorize the folk of the rural community. The American educational structure is only a framework; the meat on its bones is quite different and less palatable to young minds than we have been led to assume.

The day-to-day routine would appear to be monotonous. It starts early. Both dogs and roosters are in good voice at daybreak and help to superintend wake-up ceremonies. Another pre-breakfast sound may be that of many feet on gravel streets and walks, for good Philippine Catholics attend early mass. The yard at home and at school is probably swept each morning. There is a lack of privacy in Asian living, especially in densely settled rural areas. After breakfast women and small children go to the river for the daily laundry and bath. Men and boys may go to the fields quite early too. Their bath time at the river is probably in the early afternoon or evening after the day's field work is completed, and while the younger children are pasturing the carabao along the roadside. During the day, pantless boys "play at gambling" with stones on the plaza or in the roadway. The local sari-sari store sells a few native fruits and vegetables, local salt and muscovado sugar, rice or corn, canned sardines, warm Coca-Cola, possibly beer, and a few other items. There may be after-dark diversion by a group of *cumbancheros* (serenading minstrels).

URBAN LIVING

The Philippines bears the imprint of more than 300 years of Spanish rule and approximately half a century of American control, and this imprint is stronger in the cities and larger towns than in a more rural environment. The city and city living are not only more modern, but more Western as well. The elegance of social life in Manila is surpassed in few other places in either the Orient or the Occidental countries. A few of the Manila hotels and The Pines in Baguio rival the Conrad Hiltons or Tokyo's Imperial and Nakatsu in splendor.

Yet not all that is urban is modern, nor is it basically Western. In Manila, and to a lesser extent in Cebu, Iloilo, and Davao, there are wide modern streets, air-conditioned offices and movie theatres, modern supermarkets stocked largely with imported items, spacious homes and ranch-type bungalows of modern architecture, and other evidence of comfortable living. But in juxtaposition with these facilities one finds narrow, dusty streets and roads; crowded and unclean local markets; sidewalk venders; open-air barber shops; closely spaced, cubicle-type houses and apartments; an equally crowded Chinese section with its typical hodge-podge of living quarters, retail and service establishments (shop houses), and a Chinese school; and a host of other sights and sounds that are truly Asian.

Not all that is elaborate is solely for the tourists and the Western segment of the Philippine population. The Filipino national may live in regal splendor in a pretentious home with tiled floors, and a modern bathroom, surrounded by a private, walled or fenced yard, and staffed by numerous servants. As host he will greet his guests wearing a carefully embroidered *barong tagalog*. His wife, a most gracious hostess, will discharge her social duties dressed in an elegant, meticulously tailored gown, probably topped with a *pina terno*. His children may be bilingual or even trilingual, a result of having spoken only Tagalog with the servants, having learned good English from American teachers at a private school, and possibly having learned Spanish from the parents as well as in the classroom.

But even in the city, at least on its outskirts, there is some barrio-type living. Homes are built upon bamboo posts, with woven split-rattan (*sawali*) sidewalls, a nipa thatch or galvanized iron roof, and a split-bamboo floor. Its crowded rooms and rectangular openings in lieu of windows permit the details of family living to become

donesia and Brazil, and possibly China and India, have a comparable rate of growth. At the present rate of growth, the Philippine
population will double in a generation. And there is no evidence
that the rate will be reduced. It is understandably difficult for the
increase in production to keep pace with the increased number of
mouths to feed.

The pertinent factor in this increase is a decrease in the death
rate, not an increase in the birth rate. Greatly improved medical
facilities and techniques, along with easier access to these facilities,
have combined to affect a considerable decrease in the Philippine
death rate, especially infant mortality. Since the population is not
particularly affected by either immigration or emigration, and since
the birth rate has consistently been high and has remained reasonably constant, the substantial decrease in the death rate has caused
an accelerated growth in total population.

Social, economic, and political implications of this high growth
rate are tremendous. Since Philippine population growth is primarily a result of natural increase it adds to the infant group, and
its effects are gradually diffused through the remainder of the
population by the process of aging. The Philippines has an exceedingly young population. In 1954, more than half the population was
under 20 years of age. Great pressures have been placed on the
Philippine educational system and the labor market, and these pressures will continue. The Philippine economy has made marked
progress since 1950, but it has not kept pace with the growing labor
force. There are problems of unemployment and underemployment.
Both are likely to continue. The national goal of self-sufficiency in
food products has been handicapped more by the increased number
of mouths to feed than by the inability to increase yields or to
bring more land under food production. The housing shortage is
directly related to the rapid increase of persons to be housed. With
continued improvement in economic and social conditions it is probable that the Philippines will continue to increase in population at
a rapid rate. It is time for a hard look at population growth over
the entire country.

In most countries, possibly in all countries, the highest birth rate
is found among farm women and perhaps other rural women who

do not participate in the working force *per se*. Women who carry on some kind of economic activity in or near their home have only slightly lower fertility. In the Philippines these are the women who have a small shop or village store, who help in a family or cottage industry, or who weave cloth on a hand loom or make apparel on the family sewing machine. However, women who leave their homes during the day to work in a modern type of business or industrial establishment, to teach school at whatever level, or to work in a government office have a very much lower fertility. Hence it appears that active participation in a modern economy is likely to result in a significantly lower fertility.

For the Philippines as a whole, however, too few women are engaged in the modern sectors of the economy to affect the over-all birth rate. Most government clerks and stenographers are men. There are few women in any form of scientific work. Industry, even textile manufacture and garment factories, employ a high percentage of men. Even though half or more of the women may be reported in the working force, the great majority of them are engaged in agriculture or other home industries.

It is generally conceded that a rapidly growing population may present relatively little difficulty to an advanced economy with plenty of savings. These savings should logically seek increased investment opportunities. They can provide the funds for more capital investment, which in turn provides greater employment for the increasing population. And the growing population in turn stimulates this investment and related prosperity, for it requires more homes, more clothes, more autos and refrigerators, more toys and baby cribs—more everything. Business facilities and service industries are thus expanded, and new outlets for further investment and further employment are created.

But the growth that may aid an advanced free enterprise economy may hamper an underdeveloped nation. The Philippines has too little capital as it is. The accumulation of savings has been extremely slow, for the peasant population has low productivity and consumes virtually all that it produces. The surplus that has gone to the landlord has traditionally been used to buy more land, or for luxurious living, or for travel, or for an expensive education for his children. If it has been invested in the non-agricultural aspects of the economy, probably it has been invested in mines or shipping rather than industries that provide large numbers of employment opportunities. Only in very recent years has Philippine capital been attracted to industrial investment opportunities to any appreciable extent.

MIGRATION

Filipinos have traditionally clung to their insular homeland. Seafaring and a restless urge for migration were not among their culture traits. With a few exceptions, they stayed at home and pitted fertility against poverty, famines, and epidemics. Family ties and community interests have mitigated against any widespread movement of great numbers of people.

Overseas migration has been principally to the United States and its territories. There are small Filipino communities in some of our west coast cities, in Chicago, and elsewhere. But most American Filipinos live in Hawaii, where they make up an important segment of the population. Hawaiian Filipinos migrated primarily for employment opportunity in the 1890's and early in the twentieth century when Hawaii needed field hands for its expanding sugar industry. Most of their descendants continue to be associated with sugar production. Filipinos also have migrated to Guam, more for employment as laborers at the military base than for agricultural work. It is estimated that about 13,000 Filipinos are living in Guam, some 10,000 working on military projects.

Within the Philippines there has been some migration from the more crowded areas to some of the less densely settled regions. The Ilokanos have overflowed into nearby provinces and have gone to Mindanao, reflecting the high physiologic density of their home area on the northwest coast of Luzon and the long dry season that prevails there. Prior to the Pacific war, Ilokanos were among the leaders in some of the resettlement projects in Mindanao. In recent years many of them have crossed the mountains into the Cagayan Valley, a trend that continues today. The Cebuanos, both from Cebu and Leyte, are the principal settlers on the northern coast and the Bukidnon plateau of Mindanao. They are the agricultural settlers growing corn and coconuts, the workers on the huge Del Monte pineapple plantation and in the cannery, and the employees at the new manufacturing center at Iligan. Other Visayans and the Tagalogs have been less willing to move from the home island or province. Tagalogs have moved across the strait to northern Mindoro, but for the most part they have come from nearby Batangas and adjacent areas, rather than from the more-densely populated Central Plain.

The major postwar migration has been a rural to urban movement. The growth of Manila from a population of 623,493 in 1939, to a metropolitan urban complex approaching two million represents far greater growth than can be accounted for by the natural increase of Manila and the adjacent portions of surrounding contiguous provinces. The districts adjacent to Manila are changing from rural to semi-urban, even to urban in many ways. Manila has drawn its inhabitants from every sector of the Philippines, as well as from many countries of the world. It is now the largest city for Ilokanos and Pampangans as well as for Tagalogs and has the largest number of both Americans and Spaniards in the Orient. Filipinos migrate to Manila for educational or economic opportunity. Some of them are successful, but the percentage of unemployed is higher in Manila than for the Philippines as a whole.

4 *Languages, Religion, and Education*

T HE Philippines are a literate nation. More than three-fourths of the people can read and write, and this proportion is increasing. The Philippines reputably have the best educational system in Southeast Asia.

LINGUISTIC DIVERSITY

At least 75 native linguistic groups are recognized in the Philippines. However, about 90 percent of the population use one of the eight major dialects—Cebuano, Tagalog, Hiligayon (Ilongo), Ilokano, Bikolano, Samar-Leyte (Waray-Waray), Pampangan, or Pangasinan, in order of numerical strength. Of these eight, three are primarily Visayan in origin and five are associated with Luzon and nearby islands. About six million Cebuanos inhabit Cebu, Bohol, western and southern Leyte, northern and eastern Mindanao, eastern Negros, and southern Masbate. Possibly three million Hiligayons live on Panay, western Negros, Romblom, and the southern tip of Mindoro. There are probably one and one-half million Waray-Waray, most of them living in Samar and eastern Leyte. The Tagalogs, about five million, are numerically second to the Cebuanos. The Tagalog area is centered on Manila, but includes Marinduque Island, the Bataan Peninsula, and the coastal portions of eastern and northern Mindoro. The Bikolanos, now about two million in number, live primarily in the four provinces of the Bikol Peninsula (southeast Luzon), nearby Catanduanes, northern Masbate, and certain smaller islands. Pampangans and Pangasinans each number less than a million, and each group is centered upon the province whose name it bears. The Ilokanos, probably about three million in number, originally lived along the coast of northwest Luzon. A thrifty people, on occasion called the "Yankees of the Philippines," they have become the principal people in much of the Cagayan

Valley and some of the northern segments of the Central Plain, and some of them have migrated to Manila and Mindanao.

Linguistic boundaries are indistinct in the more densely settled lowland areas, and even less clearly defined in areas of frontier settlement. In the highlands the lesser known dialects normally predominate. Manila is a basically Tagalog city, but thousands of Cebuanos, Ilongos, Ilokanos, Bikolanos, and others now reside there. Manila has more Ilokanos than Vigan, more Bikolanos than Legaspi, and possibly more Cebuanos than Cebu City. Ilongos, Cebuanos, and some Tagalogs have migrated to Palawan. The Cotabato lowland of Mindanao is an area of frontier settlement, where one or another of the Moro dialects is the indigenous language. But many Ilokanos moved to Cotabato in prewar years. Under the late President Magsaysay's amnesty plan, "converted Huks" from Central Luzon (Pampangans and Tagalogs) were given land in Cotabato. Cebuanos have been attracted there for agricultural opportunities in recent years. Interior Mindanao is becoming a rural melting pot somewhat comparable to the linguistic hodge-podge of urban Manila.

The Tagalogs are considered the most prominent group in the Philippines. Possibly because Manila lies within the original Tagalog area, there has been more opportunity for this group to assert itself. In general, the Tagalogs are better educated, have a better literature and a somewhat richer language. Partly for these reasons, possibly in part because of political strength in the Commonwealth legislature, Tagalog was designated the national language in 1937. The present National Language, basically Tagalog, is a required course at all levels of instruction. Most of the younger Filipinos know some Tagalog.

Chinese is spoken in the Chinese communities and taught in the Chinese schools. Used only by Chinese and only in family or community groups, it is not a working language in the Philippines.

WESTERN LANGUAGES

Both English and Spanish are used, the latter only in a few areas. English is the required language of instruction at all levels beginning in the third grade. The principal newspapers and the better magazines are printed in English. Most radio programs are in

English. English (American) movies predominate, although the Philippine motion picture industry makes commercial movies in both English and the National Language. English is the language of commerce and trade and is universally used among professional people.

From a practical standpoint English is the one language that can be used throughout the Philippines. It has become the *lingua franca* of the islands. It can be used to converse with the Chinese merchant in Manila, the employees of the interisland steamer, or the bus conductor on a Mindanao highway. Using English, one can purchase basic items of food and beverage in a remote mountain community. However, Filipino English is not American English or the King's English, or even "pidgeon English." It is English words with Latin vowel sounds and some accents that are strange to the Westerner. It is Filipino English.

To be able to speak Spanish well is a mark of distinction, a social value that dates from the last century. Spanish is easily the foremost foreign language studied. (English may be a foreign tongue, but it is not considered a foreign language in the academic sense.) By action of the national congress, high school students are required to study Spanish, and most college curricula include three years of Spanish. However, it is normally spoken only in those homes with a Spanish background and is used in the business world only in those firms in which Spanish management has been retained.[1]

THE ROLE OF RELIGION

Most Filipinos are Christians and predominantly Roman Catholic. Some four percent are Moslem and about three percent are classed as pagan. Most Moslems live in Mindanao and the Sulu Archipelago, a few on southern Palawan. The pagans are primarily in the less accessible portions of the larger islands.

The only Christian country east of the Mediterranean, the Philippines has been predominantly Catholic since the beginning of the

[1] In two years of residence and travel in the Philippines, the author found it necessary to seek the assistance of a translator only once, when he went to the Manila office of "Tabacalera" to make arrangements to visit their *hacienda* and tobacco warehouses in the Cagayan Valley.

seventeenth century. This unique characteristic is the legacy of Spain and is a tribute to the zeal of early Spanish missionaries. Reportedly, spiritual evangelism was given a higher priority than commercial activities during the early years of the Spanish period. Catholicism has been fostered and enlarged in this century by missionaries from at least 10 Western countries. Of some 1300 non-Filipino priests, Spanish, American, German, Belgian, and Irish rank in the order named. Catholic orders operate more than 100 universities, colleges, and seminaries, including the University of Santo Tomas, founded in 1611; more than 400 high schools; at least 200 elementary schools; 13 hospitals and three leprosaria; and various asylums, shelters, and dispensaries. Only the Moslem population has resisted the efforts of Christian missionaries.[2]

One important difference between the Philippines and Spanish America must be stressed. For example, in colonial Mexico, immigrant Spaniards constituted fully 30 percent of the total population; in the Philippines the number was never more, and often far less, than one percent of the total. This meant that for all practical purposes, outside of Manila and a half dozen other communities, the only representative of Spanish authority was the Spanish missionary. Even more than in Mexico, the Philippines can be termed a spiritual conquest.

Catholicism has remained a dominate force in the life of the average Filipino. The parish priest is still a strong man in the community. He is present at the *fiesta,* wedding feast, christening party, and many other social events. Many of the provisions of the Civil Code in matters touching marriage and divorce coincide almost completely with corresponding legislation in Catholic Church Law. Divorce is unheard of among Filipinos. Although according to the Philippine constitution there is separation of church and state, it is difficult to keep religious instruction out of the public schools or religious direction out of politics. At the time of the 1957 national election there were full-page political announcements in Manila newspapers, paid for by the Catholic archbishops. Probably this is not surprising in a country that is more than 80 percent Catholic.

[2] Even so, there is an Ateneo de Sulu in Jolo, for there are some Catholics in Sulu Province.

MINORITY RELIGIONS

The *Philippine Independent Church,* popularly known as the Aglipayan Church, has a membership of about five percent of the population. Formed in 1902 under the leadership of a Roman Catholic priest, Gregorio Aglipay, and a journalist-politician, Isabelo de los Reyes, the Aglipayans have retained the basic format of Catholic ritual. The church differs, in part, in that the vernacular replaced Latin as the liturgical language and national heroes were added to the calendar of saints. Its strength, primarily in northern Luzon, reached a peak about 1918-1920. Since then its relative position has shown a slow but steady decline and the Catholics have shown a corresponding increase.

American Protestantism entered the Philippines at the turn of the century. Many groups are represented, most of them also sponsoring schools or hospitals, either individually or jointly under the United Church Board of New York. Notable illustrations are Brent School at Baguio and Easter Schools in Bontoc (Episcopalian), Mary Johnston Hospital in Manila (Methodist), Silliman University at Dumaguete (formerly Presbyterian, now United Board), and Central Philippine University at Iloilo (Baptist). The Protestant population has apparently stabilized at about two and one-half percent of the total population.

Islam was introduced into the Philippines before the Spaniards arrived. Moslem Filipinos, called Moros, now constitute the largest single non-Christian group in the Republic, about four percent of the population. The Moros belong to the same racial and linguistic matrix as the vast majority of the Filipinos. They are physically indistinguishable from other Filipinos, and their languages are closely related to those spoken in other parts of the country. Their chief characteristic is an almost fanatical adherence to their faith and to the cultural, social, and political traits that are related and intertwined with religious beliefs and practices. They form a vigorous, self-conscious minority whose place in the modern Philippines is significant far beyond their numbers. They occupy some of the best lands in Mindanao. There have been numerous conflicts, both legal and armed, with the national government and Christian

Filipinos. Because of banditry, it is generally considered unsafe for an outsider to travel in parts of the Moro countryside. Proud and fearless, the Moros were never conquered by the Spaniards, they were among the last people to submit to American occupation, and they did not submit to or cooperate with the Japanese. Today the Moro provinces are a regular part of the national structure, but in some respects this normality is in name only. With a feeling of kinship, at least in terms of hostility to non-Moros, these people are generally hostile to Philippine rule. Until quite recently, they had not taken advantage of educational facilities as had the Christian Filipino. In summary, the Moros are culturally advanced, numerous, and relatively cohesive. Any planning that concerns the southern Philippines cannot ignore them.

PHILIPPINE EDUCATION

The Philippine educational system is possibly the greatest single contribution of the American period. It has probably done more than any other thing to make the Philippines a unique country in Monsoon Asia. It is the only organized institution outside the family with a physical plant and paid personnel in most barrios. There is a working relationship between the barrio people and their school. The local teacher is a person to be respected. And Philippine education has great dimensions: public expenditures for education comprise the largest single item in the national budget (about half).

The system is based upon the American principles of free and universal public education, and of separation of church and state. It has a vigor and direction that holds great promise for the country. Although the philosophy is sound and the over-all organization is good, there are short-comings and some marked differences between Philippine education and its American model. The elementary work has been telescoped into seven grades instead of eight. Some teachers are poorly trained; most of them are overworked; all of them are underpaid. With few exceptions, classes are overcrowded. School-rooms are poorly equipped. There is a real need for more class-rooms; for more and better physical equipment, especially scientific supplies and maps; for larger and better libraries; and for more modern textbooks, particularly in the social sciences and some of the natural sciences. In brief, there is inadequate financial support to cope with the numbers of pupils and students that require educational training at the various levels of instruction.

The Philippines has experienced an educational renaissance since the war. Filipino people everywhere place a great importance on education. A diploma is considered a means of social, economic, and political betterment. Whereas the school enrollment, ages 7 to 17, in 1948 was 2,200,000, the 1957 enrollment in primary and secondary schools was twice that figure. By 1963 there were almost six million Filipinos enrolled in the country's schools.

Control of education is highly centralized. The over-all director is an appointed Secretary of Education, a member of the President's cabinet. With few exceptions, all at the college level, the educational activities and school interests of the Republic are under the control and supervision of the Department of Education. At sub-cabinet rank is a Director of Public Schools and a Director of Private Schools, for the Philippine educational system consists of two coordinate branches, from elementary through college.

Elementary schools are widespread even in remote mountainous regions, although many of those in the less accessible areas offer only the primary grades, one to three or one to four. Teaching at the elementary level is predominantly a feminine career, but the supervisory staff is largely made up of men. Most of the elementary teachers were trained at one of the several regional normal schools, recently renamed teachers colleges. Others were trained in the College of Education at the University of the Philippines, at Philippine Normal College, or at one of the many private colleges with teacher-education curricula.

Most of the 56 provinces have a public high school, some of them more than one. There are a few provincial trade schools and six regional agricultural schools, now called agricultural colleges. The public secondary schools, with a few exceptions, offer a general curriculum that includes vocational courses along with academic subjects.

Private schools are less widespread but are situated in all parts of the Republic. Most of them are in the cities and other larger settlements, and the emphasis is on secondary education. Most of them are associated with one or another of the Catholic religious orders. Their curriculum is more academic in character with somewhat greater emphasis on English and Spanish, and of course religion. Some parents report that they send their children to a private high school so that they will receive better instruction in the use of English.

Philippine universities, with a student enrollment of about 300,-000,[3] are both similar and dissimilar to the original American model. Manila alone has a dozen universities, two of them women's colleges. The University of Santo Tomas is older than Harvard. The University of the Philippines, the only state university until quite recently, comprises many colleges and schools and has branches or extensions beyond the central campus. It is roughly comparable to a large state university in America. The smaller church-controlled colleges or universities (such as Silliman University at Dumaguete, Ateneo de Manila, and others) are similar to a small American liberal arts college with a religious affiliation. But there is no American counterpart for the commercially operated university with an enrollment of 25,000 to 40,000 per university. (University of the East and Far Eastern University are the huge ones, but there are many others of lesser magnitude, all of them stock companies or family enterprises that are operated as commercial businesses, and return a profit to their owner or owners.) These so-called "diploma mills" have a student body composed largely of mature adults drawn from the working population. Most classes are scheduled in late afternoon or evening. Most of the faculty are part-time lecturers, often paid on a piece-meal basis. (A potential professor with a full-time position in government or industry, or a private practice in his profession, will "moonlight" for a small stipend and the honor or prestige that accompanies a university title.)

However, these large independent private universities along with the larger church-affiliated private universities in Manila have performed some useful functions. First, by the convenience of their

[3] By comparison, the 113 colleges and universities in Illinois had a combined enrollment of 253,554 in the first semester of the academic year 1962-1963.

"downtown" location they have taken much of the brunt of the rapid expansion and have diverted much of the educational traffic jam from the state university. Secondly, the success of a purely commercial university depends to a large extent upon the number of its graduates that can successfully pass the vocational or professional examinations prepared by the respective professional bodies or examining and accrediting agencies of the government. As a result these schools have produced an impressive number of competent lower- and intermediate-level trained people, such as accountants, dentists, pharmacists, and teachers. In some respects, they have filled a need where other colleges and universities have tended to leave the largest gap. Nonetheless, the idea of a commercial university that pays annual dividends to its stockholders is disconcerting to Western educators and remains contrary to Western educational philosophy.

In the final analysis, schools at all levels, both public and private, have been and continue to be overcrowded without proper regard to any rational use of the limited financial and material resources that are available for education. Hence, the original principle and the government's policy of free educational opportunity for everyone has become unrealistic. The children of the wealthier families attend the better private schools and colleges that charge higher fees. Presumably, they thereby are able to obtain a better education than their less fortunate neighbors.

5 *Production, Patterns, and Problems of Agriculture*

THE Philippine economy can be evaluated from many different points of view, but agriculture will emerge as its most important sector. About 60 percent of the gainfully employed are engaged in agricultural production. Goods of agricultural origin account for three-fourths of the value of exports. About 40 percent of the national income is a result of farming operations. A little over one-fifth of the total area is in farm land. But since late Spanish times the Philippines has not been able to feed itself.

Agriculture is not highly productive. Much of it is a family, not an individual, pursuit. It occupies a mixture of full-time and part-time workers. Much of it is subsistent in character. Approximately 40 percent of the farmers are tenants. Farm equipment ranges from primitive hand tools to power machinery. Fertilization, crop rotation, and conservation practices have shown marked improvement, but in some of the remote regions they remain almost unknown. Problems of landownership are often discouraging. Yet agricultural progress is real, and continued expansion is probable.

Problems arising from the pattern of landownership and agricultural practices differ somewhat in the various provinces and islands. But in general, tenancy is high, especially on the more level and more fertile sugar and rice lands. Specifically, it is highest in Occidental Negros and the provinces on the Central Plain of Luzon. In some cases the crop is produced by hired laborers under the direction of the owner or a farm manager. More often, these large estates are divided into smaller units and leased to individual tenants, a system not unlike the traditional share-cropping of cotton in southeastern United States. In either case absentee ownership is commonplace. Politically this system of land holding and semi-feudal cropping has negated true democratic process. It has thrived on low wages; it favors backwardness and semi-poverty. It has permitted the landholder to exercise a paternal attitude over his employees or tenants and to hold excessive political and commercial control over many people. The masses of people living in these areas are reduced to a precarious status, and the system has bred social discontent. The result has been a highly stratified society. The rise of the Hukbalahaps in central Luzon in the early 1950's was related, in part, to the agricultural system and the need for land reform.[1]

Philippine agriculture consists of plantation production for export; small-farm, cash-crop cultivation; sedentary subsistence tillage; and shifting cultivation. The last mentioned is widespread, but the least important. It is practiced principally in the rugged interiors of the larger islands and on occasion in lowland frontier areas.

Most Filipino farms are small. Average size is 10 acres, but about half the total farms are under 5 acres in size and account for only one-fifth of the total farmland. Sedentary subsistence tillage is widespread, especially in the older areas of settlement (Ilocos Coast, Central Plain, and Cebu, for example). It is an intensive hoe culture with a modest use of draft animals. Rice or corn is dominant. Some combination of sweet potatoes (*camotes*), cassava (manioc), bananas, coconuts, peanuts, tropical fruit, and vegetables complement the principal production and supplement the basic diet.

A small-farm, cash-crop farmer is primarily a commercial farmer, but he normally produces some of the family food. He will own a carabao and a few crude implements. His cash crop may be coconuts, sugar cane, abaca, tobacco, coffee, fruit, or vegetables—probably more than one of these. In addition, he grows some rice or corn, probably bananas or cassava, possibly table vegetables. He may have a fruit tree or two solely for home use, a few chickens, and a pig or pigs. There is no sharp division between the small commercial farm and a truly subsistent one.

The cultivation of large land holdings for export products was developed in Spanish times and with Spanish capital. Under this system, sometimes called *hacienda* agriculture on Luzon and in the

---

[1] For an expansion of this paragraph see the author's "Problems of Land Ownership in the Philippine Islands," *Economic Geography,* Vol. 28, 1952, pp. 31-36.

Visayans, the products were—and still are—sugar cane, coconuts, and in a few areas tobacco or abaca. Some lands are regularly planted to food crops for the *hacienda* laborers. In Mindanao and nearby smaller islands the large estate is more properly called a plantation. It was developed at a later date with American, or occasionally with European or Filipino, capital. Often it is devoted to a single product: pineapples, rubber, ramie, or abaca. More likely there are two or more cash crops. One scientific plantation on Basilan has 250-750 acres each in coconuts, rubber, abaca, and coffee, raises more than 1200 pepper plants, has experimented with cacao and vanilla, grazes beef cattle on kudzu pasture under coconuts, and supplies both chickens and pigs to the local market.

FOOD CROPS AND SUBSISTENCE AGRICULTURE

As agriculture dominates the Philippine economy, rice production dominates Philippine agriculture. However, corn supplants rice as the staple food in the diet on certain of the central and southern islands, and the sweet potato is the principal food in the mountains of northern Luzon and some other upland areas. Locally, one of the commercial crops (sugar cane, coconuts, abaca, tobacco, rubber, or pineapples) may be more important or cover a larger acreage than food crops. But in only 3 of the 53 provinces (Laguna, Quezon, and Davao) is the acreage of commercial crops greater than that of food crops.

Rice, of which there are hundreds of varieties, is easily the most important crop. Over 70 percent of the population depends primarily upon rice for food. Approximately five million acres (about 40 percent of the cultivated land) are planted annually to rice. Primary rice-producing regions are the Central Plain of Luzon, the Panay Plain, the Bikol Region, and parts of the Cagayan Valley. Culture methods are similar to those of other Southeast Asian lands. Wet-lowland or paddy culture is most prevalent and probably supplies 75 percent of the total crop.

Most irrigation in the Philippines is simply the control of rainfall by a series of canals and ditches with associated contouring and dikes. The system is designed to control or regulate the amount of water necessary for proper growth of the crop. The world-famous

Ifugao rice terraces in the mountains of northern Luzon are the classic and colorful illustration of this kind of gravity control of irrigation water, but irrigation by this method is commonplace almost everywhere that rice is grown. Private river-diversion systems were built on some extensive estates (*haciendas*) in Spanish time. Within the present century several large irrigation plants were constructed by the colonial or Commonwealth government. In 1952 a pump irrigation program was initiated, using water from Laguna de Bay (a fresh-water lake), from permanent streams, or from shallow wells. In most cases this program provides supplementary irrigation during the dryer part of the year, either to permit increased yields of the crop or to provide for a second crop of rice in an area where a second crop would not otherwise be possible. Within the past several years a few large irrigation dams on major rivers have been constructed. For example, Magat Dam on a tributary of the Cagayan, opened in 1957, is more than 600 feet long and its water is used to irrigate more than 50,000 acres of rice land.

Upland rice culture is widespread, but of distinctly lesser importance than paddy culture. It is of two types. "Slash and burn" or *kaingin* methods are still prevalent among some of the primitive groups in mountainous areas and among some Christian Filipinos in frontier areas. Only a minor portion of Philippine rice is grown by this method. Although slash and burn agriculture is prohibited by the Bureau of Forestry, the law is seldom enforced; so the practice remains as a part of Philippine subsistence agriculture. More widespread and more important is the normal dry or upland planting of rice on lands or soils that are not suited to paddy culture. No dikes or other water control is used. Methods, then, are similar to those of Midwestern farmers with a small acreage of middle-latitude small grains. Upland rice yields are generally lower than that of lowland varieties and paddy culture.

The Philippines is on the margin of rice self-sufficiency. Yields per acre are low and fluctuate widely, depending upon culture methods, climatic conditions, or other factors. Historically the country has been a rice importer. Government policy has stressed the goal of self-sufficiency in basic food commodities, particularly rice. This goal (self-sufficiency in rice) was attained for the first time in

1958. In the past decade, the Philippines has never imported more than seven percent of the rice consumed. Most of the Philippines has a distinct dry season so that multiple rice cropping is not possible. Two paddy crops are common only on the Bicol Plain of southeastern Luzon and a few other small areas that are also on the eastern coast of the Republic. Double cropping of rice is just becoming significant on the Central Plain of Luzon, the principal rice area of the Republic. The expansion of rice acreage, both paddy and replant varieties, in frontier areas, and the development of higher-yielding varieties are equally significant in permitting the country to produce its normal rice needs.

Corn, or maize, is the second most important food crop in the Philippines. More than 2.5 million acres (about 15 percent of the cultivated area) is planted to corn. Over most of the country it is a secondary or minor crop, but in Cebu, Eastern Negros, parts of Leyte, the Bukidnon Plateau, and the northern coast of Mindanao it is the primary food staple. It is also the primary cereal on the sandy alluvial soils of the middle Cagayan Valley of Luzon. Corn is the security crop in frontier areas where irrigated rice fields have not yet been prepared. It has replaced abaca on those mosaic-infested plantations along Davao Gulf.

About 25 percent of the population lives chiefly on corn, normally coarsely ground meal that is prepared and eaten much as rice is used in other areas. Depending on physical conditions, as many as four crops per year are grown. Yields are low. Cropping practices vary greatly. In some areas it is the basic crop. In other areas it is grown as an important subsidiary to upland rice, as in Batangas. In most *kaingin* agriculture, corn is the first crop and may be intercropped with rice or root crops. In Sulu Province it is intercropped with peanuts and cassava. Throughout the Philippines corn is a household garden crop, most often harvested in the milk stage and eaten as corn-on-the-cob. Modern hybrids have failed abysmally in the Philippines. Apparently, Western hybrids are totally unsuited to tropical conditions, and no productive Philippine hybrids have yet been developed.

Lesser food crops such as sweet potatoes and bananas, are widespread and locally quite important. The former is most important in

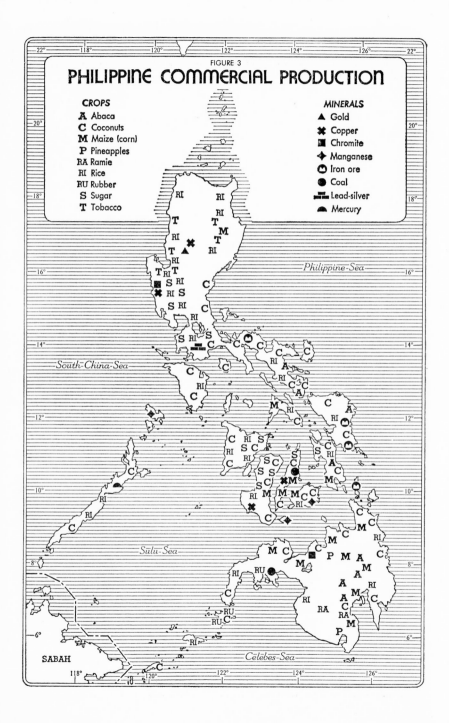

FIGURE 3

PHILIPPINE COMMERCIAL PRODUCTION

CROPS
A Abaca
C Coconuts
M Maize (corn)
P Pineapples
RA Ramie
RI Rice
RU Rubber
S Sugar
T Tobacco

MINERALS
▲ Gold
✖ Copper
▦ Chromite
◆ Manganese
◉ Iron ore
● Coal
━ Lead-silver
🜨 Mercury

hillside and mountain agriculture. Sweet potatoes have become the staple item in many remote areas in mountainous northern Luzon. Bananas, including cooking bananas, are grown throughout the country except extreme northern Luzon, normally in garden-like patches around the farmstead. Cassava or manioc for food or for starch is more important in the southern islands than on Luzon. Mungo beans and peanuts are dry-season crops or are intercropped with corn. Eggplant and green beans are the more widespread of the common vegetables. Tomatoes, cucumbers, melons, and various tropical vegetables may be locally and seasonally important. The Trinidad Valley in the mountains north of Baguio is a significant producer of superior mid-latitude vegetables for the Baguio and Manila markets. It has established a pattern and a prestige that has encouraged a similar type of horticulture around some urban centers and in a few highland communities in the southern islands.

There is a great variety of fruit, of which the mango and papaya are the most prevalent and the most important. Native pineapples, the mandarin orange, pili nuts, lanzones, and a variety of other tropical fruit are marketed locally in season. Both foreign enterprise and domestic capital have fostered an infant coffee industry that is of increasing importance, particularly in Batangas and parts of Mindanao. The principal fruit and vegetable area is near Manila in Bulacan, Cavite, and Batangas.

COMMERCIAL AGRICULTURE

Traditionally a large segment of Philippine agriculture has been geared to commercial products, principally for shipment to American markets. (See Figure 3.) Agriculture is responsible for 80 percent of the country's export. Sugar cane, coconuts, abaca, and pineapples are grown primarily for export, secondarily for Philippine markets. The production of tobacco, rubber, coffee, and ramie is commercial agriculture, but these products are marketed principally or solely within the Philippines.

Sugar. For almost a half century the production of sugar cane has occupied a dominant position in the economic structure of the Philippines. Originally processed in crude mills using antiquated methods, the product was sold or bartered as muscovado or panocha sugar with production limited to local or regional demands. After the introduction of centrifugal mills (1914-1920) the industry was reoriented toward the export market, and production increased rapidly. More than a million tons have been processed each year since 1920, except for the period from 1942 through 1950. There was little sugar produced during the period of Japanese occupation, and from 1945 to 1950 the industry was faced with the problems of re-construction and re-establishment, both in the field and in the factory.

Recent production has averaged a little less than 1.5 million tons annually. Only Cuba, Brazil, India, the United States, and possibly mainland China produce more sugar from cane than does the Philippines. Commercial sugar production in the Philippines is con-centrated principally in central Luzon and on Negros with smaller amounts from Panay, Cebu, and Leyte. Negros accounts for more than 60 percent of the tonnage produced.

The sugar industry has heavy seasonal labor requirements and, historically, has been closely associated with areas of a relatively dense population or with regions where labor can be imported per-manently or periodically to supply the need. Labor supply has never been a real problem in Philippine sugar districts. It has been neces-sary to recruit labor from other islands only for the Negros industry, and in this case only in moderate numbers. In the Philippines the use of modern machinery in cultivating and harvesting has devel-oped slowly. The larger planters have tractors and other mechanized equipment, but thousands of small planters must continue to rely upon the carabao for their source of power. A tractor pool, operated by the *central*, is a postwar innovation, and custom plowing is gain-ing significance.

Probably no commodity in international trade is more subject to political control than sugar. Only about 10 percent of the total an-nual production of 60 million tons is sold on the world market without the aid of governmental regulation, such as preferential tariffs, quotas, or other controls. Philippine sugar is and has been directly tied to the American market. Philippine colonial status in pre-World War II years fostered this relationship and provided the background for its continuance. Under the terms of the Philippine

Trade Act of 1946 and the United States Sugar Act, the Philippines was permitted to sell (in the United States) 952,000 short tons of sugar annually, initially under especially favorable conditions. The Laurel-Langley Agreement (December, 1954) revised this figure upward. With the reallocation of the Cuban quota in 1960, the quota for Philippine planters and processors was increased by an additional 70,000 tons. Currently the Philippines supplies the United States with more than a million tons yearly.

The Philippine sugar industry operates with reasonable effectiveness despite a series of interrelated problems or limitations that collectively keep the industry somewhat marginal in character. The principal handicaps are associated with soil improvement, soil conservation, fertilization, and moisture control. Secondly, since Philippine labor costs have increased, greater over-all mechanization of cane production is desirable. A third group of problems lies within the general realm of cane breeding, disease control, and insect control. An effective program of basic agricultural research for the entire industry is yet to be developed. Fourth, in some areas agricultural land use mitigates against a competitive sugar industry. There are too many small planters, and many of them are inefficient cane producers. The operator of a vest-pocket farm is not a satisfactory cane producer in the Philippines. Finally, more efficient utilization of by-products is necessary for the development of a truly competitive industry. Nonetheless, fewer acres now produce as much or more sugar than was produced on larger acreages in the period before World War II. The higher acre yields are a result of increased use of fertilizer, some improvement of seed stock, more efficient agricultural techniques (i.e., more mechanization), and some restriction of production to the better cane lands.[2]

Coconuts. The Philippines is the world's foremost producer of coconut products, with more than 40 percent of the world total. In acreage planted and in number of people gainfully employed, coconuts consistently have been the leading Philippine cash crop. About

[2] Additional information about trends and status of the Philippine sugar industry may be obtained from the author's "Trends in Philippine Sugar Production," *Economic Geography,* Vol. 14, 1938, pp. 154-158, and his "The Philippine Sugar Industry: Status and Problems," *Journal of Geography,* Vol. 60, 1961, pp. 5-9.

a million hectares (2.5 million acres) are planted to coconuts, which represents almost two-thirds of the export crop area and 15 percent of the total area for all crops. More than four million people are engaged directly or indirectly in the coconut industry.

Commercial production of coconuts extends from central Luzon southward, with southeastern Luzon the area of densest planting. Most recent expansion of the industry is in southeastern Mindanao. There are few coconuts in northern, especially northwestern Luzon, presumably because of the greater typhoon frequency in northern areas and a longer dry season along the Ilocos Coast. Most coconuts are situated at low altitudes and near the coast. Coconut lands are often planted to other crops when the trees are young, and rice or corn may be planted in an old coconut grove with open areas resulting from the removal of diseased or storm-damaged trees.

The copra industry of the Philippines consists primarily of small enterprises. Most coconut groves are plots of less than five hectares (12.5 acres). Large plantations are comparatively few and are situated chiefly in the more recently developed sections of the southern islands. Even though the Philippines is the foremost copra-producing country (about a million metric tons annually), the product generally is of poor quality. This situation is explained in part by the fact that the industry is in the hands of small operators, many of whom use substandard methods of cultivation, drying, and marketing. Much good copra is spoiled as a result of faulty storage, either in buildings or in ships. Nonetheless, some good copra is produced in the Philippines.

Both coconut oil and desiccated coconut are produced, the former primarily for domestic uses. Desiccated coconut is almost totally for export. Although there are less than a half-dozen plants, the amount is truly significant. One single enterprise employs some 2000 workers in the combined field and factory operation. Coconut oil, the principal Philippine cooking fat, is also used in quantity in the manufacture of soap, vegetable shortening, and related products. There are two major plants, both subsidiaries of international establishments, that produce and use most of the coconut oil extracted. But there are many small oil mills and soap factories. Both copra and dessicated coconut are produced in greater quantities than before the war, but the coconut oil industry has not been rebuilt to its prewar capacity. The Philippine coconut industry has probably passed its peak. Competition in vegetable oils is becoming more severe, partly as a result of the bumper soybean crops of the American Midwest. In addition, some Philippine areas are afflicted with *kadang-kadang,* a mysterious disease of the coconut tree that scientists have not brought under control.

Abaca. Prior to World War II, the Philippines possessed a virtual monopoly on abaca, known commercially as Manila hemp, and supplied 95 percent of the world total. Production of this premium hard fiber has since declined, until Philippine production is no more than two-thirds of the prewar total, a result of disease in some areas, generally higher labor costs throughout the country, and increased production elsewhere, particularly in Central America. Abaca is now the third-ranking agricultural export, but the Philippines still supplies more than 90 percent of the world's supply.

Requiring moisture throughout the year, abaca production is principally along the eastern coasts and secondly in the interior valleys of Mindanao. Historically the Bicol Peninsula of Luzon, Leyte, and Samar have been abaca areas, where abaca and coconuts were major cash crops in small farming operations. Before 1941, Japanese immigrants developed plantation abaca in southeastern Mindanao (the Davao area) and supplied as much as 40 percent of the export. Repatriation of the Japanese and postwar land-holding readjustments have again emphasized the role of the small farmer who grows abaca as a cash crop along with corn or rice, bananas, and vegetables as food crops. In recent years the inability to control disease in the old Japanese plantation areas along Davao Gulf has resulted in the nearly total elimination of abaca from coastal Mindanao. These former abaca lands are now planted to corn and coconuts, and newly opened lands in the interior of the island have become progressively more important for abaca.

Although Manila hemp has enjoyed and continues to have a world market, its future is subject to considerable speculation. The declining role of the Philippine industry reflects generally increased Philippine labor costs, the effects of abaca mosaic and the costs of disease control in Mindanao, competition of abaca from other areas of the world, competition of other fibers (particularly some of the synthetics), and occasional severe typhoon damage to the banana-like plant in Luzon, Samar, and Leyte. Philippine abaca will never regain its prewar position in the domestic economy.[3]

Tobacco. Tobacco production is the oldest industrialized agricultural enterprise in the country, antedating sugar, coconuts, and abaca as a major product of commerce and trade. Introduced into the Philippines from Mexico by Spanish missionaries during the sixteenth century, the plant proved adaptable to the soil and climate of the Islands. Good quality cigar tobacco has been grown in the Philippines for almost two centuries. Since 1950 aromatic cigarette tobacco has been produced for the postwar domestic cigarette industry.

Tobacco is grown, at least in small amounts, in every province, but two districts are responsible for almost all of the truly commercial production. The middle Cagayan Valley of northeastern Luzon has been the leading area for cigar filler, an importance that dates from the government monopoly of the Spanish period. It is a dry-season crop, with corn planted during the wet season, on sandy alluvial soils that are too porous for efficient rice production. The Ilocos Coast of northwestern Luzon has become the principal area for cigarette tobacco. Theoretically, tobacco is the second crop on rice lands in the Ilocos Provinces, but the "second crop" has become the first crop in terms of income produced per acre. It is the second crop only in terms of the date of planting.

Tobacco production, stimulated by high price supports on cigarette tobacco, is now greater than during the prewar peak years of 1934-1938, but exports have not attained the prewar figure. Spain is the principal foreign market for Philippine leaf tobacco (cigar filler) and the United States (Hawaii) is the principal importer of Philippine cigars. Although tobacco cultivation occupies less than 200,000

---

[3] For a good treatment of Philippine abaca see J. E. Spencer's "Abaca in the Philippines," *Economic Geography,* Vol. 27, 1951, pp. 95-106, and his "The Abaca Plant and Its Fiber, Manila Hemp," *Economic Botany,* Vol. 7, 1953, pp. 195-213.

acres, the industry supplies about 20 percent of the total income of the Bureau of Internal Revenue.[4]

Minor commercial crops. Several lesser agricultural products are grown for export or domestic processing. One huge pineapple enterprise on Mindanao, a 15,000 acre scientific plantation and associated cannery, is designed totally for the export market. Rubber, so important in Malaya and Indonesia, is the principal product of some half dozen large plantations. The Philippine rubber industry can use all domestic rubber produced. Maguey, a type of sisal fiber, is exported in small amounts, and bananas have been shipped to Japan on an experimental basis. Fostered largely by import controls, coffee plantings have increased markedly in the past decade. Ramie, an annual fiber plant, has gained local importance in Cotabato and Davao provinces (Mindanao).

THE ANIMAL INDUSTRY

Work animals are essential to the largely unmechanized agriculture of the Philippines and therefore to its economy. Rice production, especially, requires animal power; hence, the importance of the carabao, a powerful, docile beast that can effectively work the muddy rice paddies and can forage on cogan grass (*Imperata cylindrica*), the principal grass cover of the Philippines and one that is unpalatable to cattle and most other livestock. The carabao population is heaviest in rice and sugar cane areas, lowest in coconut and abaca regions.

Cattle are used principally for food, secondly for draft purposes. All cities and many towns have meat stalls in their public markets. A modest cattle industry has been developed on the Bukidnon Plateau, parts of the Cagayan Valley, and some of the smaller islands (Masbate and Basilan). Bullocks are used as draft animals in the pineapple fields of Mindanao and to some extent in the Ilocos Provinces. There is no dairy industry, except for a few small-scale dairy farms near Manila.

Philippine horses are really sturdy ponies with great strength and

[4] See the author's "Tobacco Production in The Philippines," *Transactions of the Illinois State Academy of Science,* Vol. 52, 1959, pp. 33-44 for a fuller treatment of the Philippine tobacco industry.

resistance to disease. Historically the carriage draft animal through-out the Islands, they still are used to pull carts of various designs (the traditional *calesas,* and *carratellas*) in many rural areas and some of the towns and cities. In general, horse-carts have been re-placed by the ubiquitous jeepney.

Swine are commonplace. There are no hog farms, but most farmers and many village or town residents keep a pig or two. The family pig is a scavenger animal whether tied to a corner of the house, kept in a small bamboo enclosed pen, or permitted to range at large. It is fed kitchen wastes, rice bran mash, weeds and grass from the rice paddy, sweet potato vines, or any other material that is available and edible. It is slaughtered at both abattoirs and home sites, and sold in city and village market stalls. Roast pig, *lechon,* is a must at any village *fiesta* or other festive occasion.

There are a few chicken farms near Manila and a few duck farms along the shores of Laguna de Bay. In both cases the poultry is kept primarily for eggs, secondly for the poultry market. A few chickens or other fowl, like swine, are commonplace among rural and village families. Therefore, fowl compete with pork on middle- and upper-class tables, especially in the Visayan Islands.

AN EVALUATION

Modern agricultural production is a result of the application of knowledge derived from basic research to problems of human nutri-tion and welfare. The agricultural producers in the industrialized countries are highly sophisticated groups who have taken full ad-vantage of available knowledge and tools. Production has steadily increased, while manpower requirements and unit costs have simul-taneously declined. The secret of this success story lies in men rather than in machines.

In the Philippines, the great barrier is, and for a substantial period in the future will continue to be, the lack of a sufficient number of nationals willing and able to participate in basic agricultural re-search and to apply the results of that research to the immediate problems of the industry and nation. Progress on a united front will depend upon the rapidity with which Filipinos are trained and will accept the varied responsibilities related to agricultural production, distribution, marketing, and complete utilization of agricultural resources. Friendly nations can help to solve, but cannot resolve, the problems that arise. Massive application of modern technology over wide areas of an underdeveloped area is impossible in practice. Intermediate steps or "plateaus of progress" are necessary.

The United States technical assistance program has contributed much, and generally this aid has been received with gratitude and appreciation. Especially important in the assistance program has been agricultural education. Training abroad for special purposes is vitally important; training in the homeland is equally important. Both have been emphasized in the Philippine program. However, a broad base for economic growth and social progress is developed at home, through interrelated programs designed to prepare increasing numbers of people to respond to the problems of the present and the demands of the future. This broad base is not developed in the short span of a particular aid program, but over a period of decades by a number of dedicated individuals working in a friendly environment, with a sympathetic government, and for an appreciative agricultural population. In general, the place to study techniques and procedures of tropical agriculture is in the tropics, rather than at an agricultural experiment station in the middle latitudes.

The Philippine economy is and will continue to be cast upon an agricultural base, even after the current impetus to the expansion of manufacturing has materially expanded that phase of the economy. The country is not and never will be an agricultural paradise, but it is a country with considerable agricultural potential, with some aspects of this potential grossly underdeveloped, if not completely untapped.

T HE Philippines possesses a variety of mineral resources, but most of them are markedly limited in either quality or quantity, or both. Although mineral production is on a relatively small scale when compared to major world producers, output is sufficient to place the Republic near the front in mineral production among her Southeast Asian neighbors. Among them, only Indonesia and Malaysia have greater mineral wealth, this because of the great petroleum and tin resources. More than 50 Philippine mining companies have published an annual report in recent years. Stocks of almost half of them are traded on the Manila Stock Exchange, one of them on the New York Stock Exchange. Total mineral production, valued at $120 million annually, is exceeded only by the agricultural mainstays of sugar and copra. Eighty percent of Philippine minerals are produced for export. Many mining companies were developed with American capital and a few of them have Western managers, superintendents, or engineers. Several of them have close marketing ties with United States firms.

PRECIOUS METALS

Gold and silver. Gold mining is the oldest commercial mining industry in the Philippines, having developed early in the present century. In 1940 there were 42 operating mines with an annual production valued at $38 million. Gold mining was easily the leading mineral industry, and the Philippines ranked sixth among gold-producing countries. Most of the output was and still is from the geologically complex mountain area of northern Luzon, the Baguio mining area. The product is shipped to the United States and secondly to the United Kingdom.

Post-World War II operations have been markedly less, but the Philippines is still the eighth-ranking country and the leading gold producer in Asia. The failure to regain the prewar position reflects the fact that gold recovery from the more prevalent low grade ore brings small return to the operator, at best. With the wartime loss and damage to mines and equipment and as a result of higher postwar wages, marginal producers either have not redeveloped their holdings or have been forced to close. Of the 14 operating mines in the peak postwar year of 1953 less than a half dozen have continued through the past decade. Any significant expansion is unlikely.

Silver is not mined separately, but is recovered along with the gold as frequently the two are naturally alloyed. The only exception is a lead-silver deposit in Batangas.

BASE METALS AND FERRO-ALLOYS

The commercially mined base metals include iron, chromite, manganese, copper, lead, zinc, mercury, and nickel. Among these, iron ore ranks first in both quantity and value. Chromite is of greatest strategic importance. Copper production has expanded most rapidly within the past decade. Mercury and nickel are the result of recent developments.

Iron Ore. Philippine iron ore constitutes the principal source of foreign ore for Japanese steel mills and ranks second to gold in value of Philippine mineral production. Reserves total 35 million tons of marketable and high-grade ore (55-60 percent ore) and more than a billion tons of medium-low-grade lateritic ore (47 percent ore).[1]

The existence of modest deposits of iron ore has been known for centuries, and deposits near Manila were worked for a local iron industry as early as 1750, probably even in pre-Spanish times. Modern production for the Japanese market began in the middle thirties, and in both 1939 and 1940 exports exceeded a million tons. Postwar redevelopment was slow, largely because of strained Japanese-Philippine relations, and the 1939 production was not equalled until 1952. Present production is about a million and a quarter tons annually, 97 percent exported to Japan. The chief producing mines are in southeastern Luzon, southeastern Samar, and Marinduque Island. (See Figure 3.)

The outstanding reserves are in northeastern Mindanao and nearby

[1] Philippine Bureau of Mines, Information Circular No. 19, "Mineral Resources of the Philippines," 1958, pp. 17-18.

small islands, constituting one of the larger ore bodies of the world. Unfortunately, these lateritic ores contain quantities of aluminum, chromium, and nickel that make refining difficult and costly. For this reason the reserves are little used. Some of them, on Dinagat Island, are beginning to be utilized for their nickel content, but are not yet competitive in the steel industry.

Philippine *chromite* is of special interest, because the United States uses 35 percent of the world's chrome—and 99 percent of its needs are supplied by imports. Commercial chromite production in the Philippines began in 1935. By 1939 the Philippines was the world's fifth ranking producer, and 98 percent of the output was shipped to the United States. Mines are near the coast, and chromite production was resumed in quantity immediately after the war. Annual exports have averaged well over 500,000 tons of ore and 30,000 tons of concentrates for the past decade. In recent years only the U.S.S.R. and the Republic of South Africa have produced more chrome than the Philippines. Except for token shipments to Japan, Spain, and Canada all Philippine chrome is shipped to the United States.

Chromite is found in western, northeastern, and southeastern Luzon, southern Samar, eastern and northern Mindanao, Palawan, and elsewhere. Reserves are sufficient to last for many years at the present rate of mining. Commercial production is primarily from Zambales Province, with limited amounts shipped from Misamis Oriental (Northern Mindanao). Most Philippine chromite ore is lower-grade refractory chrome, of which the Philippines is the world's major producer and supplies 85 percent of U. S. needs. The country ranks sixth in the export of metallurgical chrome.

Manganese deposits are small, and the ore is often of low quality. It was mined by small operators in Buswanga, Bohol, Siquijor, Ilocos Norte, and elsewhere in prewar years and in most of these same areas more recently. Principal markets are the United States and Japan, although there have been shipments to Great Britain and Hong Kong. Peak production was in 1938, maximum postwar shipments in 1950 and 1959. It appears that Philippine manganese is competitive only at periods of peak demand on the world market.

Copper deposits of varying quality are known to exist on Luzon,

Negros, Cebu, and Samar, but recent commercial production has been confined to two mines, one in the mountains of northern Luzon, the other in central Cebu. The Luzon mine, in many years the largest copper-producing mine in the Orient, and until recently the only large producer in the Philippines, ships all of its products to smelters at Tacoma, Washington.

Since 1955 a modern flotation-process mill using low-grade ore (1.1 to 1.8 percent) has been operating at Toledo, Cebu. Known reserves will last 20 to 30 years. Concentrates are shipped to Japan under a long-term contract, and secondly to the United States. At capacity this may be the largest copper mine in the Far East. Newest developments and possibilities are at Sipalay in southwestern Negros (10 million tons of one percent ore); on Samar, where large deposits of 1.5 percent ore have been discovered; and on the Zambales Peninsula of Luzon. Annual Philippine production (1957-1960) averages 50,000 tons. Of Asian countries, only Japan produces more copper. The future of copper in the Philippines is bright.

Lesser base metals. Lead, zinc, and mercury are produced in the Philippines. Lead and zinc are associated with some gold ores, except for the one lead-silver mine in Batangas. The first and only mercury mine in the Philippines and the second in Asia is on Palawan. It began operations in 1955. Annual production is more than 3000 flasks valued at 1.5 million pesos. The first nickel production (45 tons of nickel-platinum concentrate) was shipped to Japan in 1961.

ENERGY RESOURCES

The Philippine economy has been handicapped by limited production of mineral fuels. In several areas, geologic structures appear favorable for *petroleum* deposits. Petroleum traces and seepages had been reported on several islands. Systematic surveys were conducted and test wells drilled, but not until 1961 were producing strata found. In 1961 production was only 5000 barrels, and in 1962 it dropped to 2000 barrels. Therefore, the new Philippine petroleum refineries remain dependent upon imported oil, principally from Indonesia.

Although *coal*-bearing strata are widely distributed, proven reserves are limited. Seams are thin and broken by surface movement; thus mining costs are high. Philippine coal is high in volatile matter. There is no coal of coking quality to complement the huge iron-ore reserves. Producing mines are in Cebu and southern Mindanao, both far from the Manila manufacturing district. Historically, coal was imported from Australia and Japan, primarily for the railways. In the postwar years, Philippine industry and commerce have turned to oil and hydroelectric power. (The Manila Railroad is now entirely dieselized.) Current production of coal averages about 150,000 tons annually.

In this area of mountainous terrain with a high annual rainfall, potential *hydroelectric power* is high. Estimates range as high as 1,500,000 kilowatts. But most of the better power sites are away from the principal markets, so development has been slow. Between 1915, when the first hydroelectric plant was built, and the outbreak of the Pacific War in 1941, 26 plants were placed in operation, but their total capacity was less than half the aggregate installed capacity (72,448 kilowatts) of the 217 public utility plants then in the Islands.

Demand for electric power in the Philippines has been growing rapidly. Postwar developments have been significant, though modest by Western standards. The first large one, a reconstruction and expansion of a prewar installation about 30 miles from Manila, initially supplied much of the power used in Manila and lesser amounts to towns in Batangas and Laguna. It will be supplemented by the 200,000 kilowatt plant on the Angat River in Bulacan, under construction in 1964, and by the 120,000 kilowatt Marikina multipurpose project on the outskirts of Manila.

In northern Luzon the Agno River developments are the most notable. The Ambuklao plant (75,000 kilowatts) was completed in 1955 and the Binga project (100,000 kilowatts) in 1960. The former was designed primarily to supply the fuel-short Baguio mining district, but it also was tied in with Manila and the Lingayen Gulf area. Binga production feeds into the rapidly expanding power net of central and northern Luzon. Both the Binga and the Angat installations are financed by loans from the World Bank.

The idea of a power plant at scenic Maria Cristina Falls near Lake Lanao in Mindanao was first conceived in the early thirties.

In terms of physical potential it is the most ideal power site in the country. Since it was opened in 1953 as a 25,000 kilowatt installation, its capacity has been doubled. It provides the basic power needs for a small steel mill, two fertilizer factories, a cement plant, a flour mill, a chemical plant, and several other small industries, all of them built since 1953 and all of them badly needed in the new Republic. A new 100,000 kilowatt plant at a second site on the Argus River is under serious consideration by the National Power Corporation (1962). Power output has increased an average of 14 percent per year since 1950, and installed capacity is now more than 650 thousand kilowatts.

NON-METALLIC MINERALS

Other than the energy resources, the non-metallic minerals known and used include sand and gravel, clay, building stone, limestone, salt, certain fertilizer minerals, asphalt, glass sand, gypsum, marble, pyrites, and sulphur. Most of them are unimportant even in the local economy. Clay is used for a backyard pottery industry in many localities. Its products are brick, tile, and domestic items (pots, jars, charcoal stoves). Local sand and gravel supplies the construction needs in most areas. The one major glass factory uses local silica sand, primarily. Rock asphalt from Leyte has been used in road building. Gypsum was produced between 1948 and 1953. Local building stone includes coral blocks, limestone blocks, and a local "adobe" that is simply consolidated volcanic ash. Salt is obtained from the evaporation of sea water during the dry season. It is an important industry along the shore of Manila Bay. Guano in small amounts is obtained from caves on Bohol and elsewhere. Pyritic sulphur is sold to the National Development Corporation's steel mill in Mindanao.

THE MINERAL ENDOWMENT

No nation yet knows the exact magnitude of its fuel resources or its metallic minerals. The mere existence of minerals does not guarantee economic utility. Estimating reserves is a complicated task. Studies of Philippine reserves naturally have been most intensive in regard to products for which home mineral needs have been greatest (coal, for example) and those for which export opportunities are clear (such as chromium and gold). Iron-ore reserves are not specifically known, and the copper deposits have not been fully evaluated. Experts agree that the mineral potential of the Philippines has not been fully tapped, probably not even adequately explored.

There is little to give either continuity or regionality to the inventory of Philippine mineral resources. Minerals are where one finds them. The freeing of mineral wealth from the rock or foreign material has given rise to an important industry, but as techniques change or new ore bodies are found, it tends to shift or migrate. Production in near-marginal operations is dependent upon world conditions. Competition is keen in some cases. But on the whole the Philippines has been exceedingly fortunate in the variety of mineral resources within the country and the quantity of some of them. In our changing world the mineral supply is not static; it is, rather, a function of the ratio between supply and demand. Then too, in the Philippines, mineral production reflects national politics as well as economic and geologic factors.

O FTEN a simple two-fold classification of industry is envisioned, namely, processing and manufacturing. Historically, Philippine industry consisted primarily of processing plants that were engaged in the simple transformation of one or more primary materials in the strict sense of the word. More recently, a greater number of plants qualify as manufacturing industries—that is, they use several, possibly many, raw materials and produce a finished product or products rather than semi-finished goods.

For most nations, modern industrialization is the eventual goal. The Philippines is no exception. The process of transition from an agricultural nation to an industrialized state is not easy. Techniques and procedures may vary, and attendant experiences are frequently painful. The Philippine Republic may never become a truly industrialized nation, but it is well into a transitional period from an agrarian society to a partially industrialized economy. The chief manufacturing categories are foods and beverages, clothing, tobacco products, metal fabrication, and transportation equipment.

Industrialization is spreading in Asia. To some countries, such as Japan, a large manufacturing industry is necessary to continued national existence. To some countries with a reasonable variety of industrial raw materials and a huge home market, such as India, the development of large manufacturing plants is a logical expectation. Some countries with a paucity of mineral fuels and no great variety of other requisites of modern industry, such as Thailand, may never attain a significant manufacturing economy. The Philippines fits none of these categories. Nonetheless, whenever there is a change from an essentially rural society consisting of a small majority of large and wealthy landowners along with a great majority of unschooled "tillers of the soil" to a society that consists of a small group of entrepreneurs with capital to invest and a large group of literate wage-earners, there is an attendant basic change, or at least a radical revision, of long-established institutions. There is both economic and cultural change; there is a probable change in philosophy, the way of life of the people. The Philippines is in this period of transition. Whatever will be the final product, the decade of 1950-1960 may well have been the most significant period in Philippine economic history.

PATTERN OF MANUFACTURING, 1945-1950 [1]

Manufacturing was an insignificant activity in the Philippines prior to the outbreak of the Pacific War. Despite a vigorous commercial development during the American regime, there was no corresponding industrial evolution. In the prewar period and in the immediate postwar years, manufacturing consisted principally of three kinds of establishments. First, there were, and still are, hundreds of small home or family industries—pottery, shoes (wooden clogs and abaca sandals), weaving industries of various kinds, furniture (both hardwood and rattan), embroidery work, milling of corn and rice, musovado and panocha sugar, and bolo factories.

Secondly, there were larger plants that processed agricultural, mineral, or forest products, primarily for export; and often they were financed by foreign capital. Included in this group were the centrifugal sugar mills, some of them with associated distilleries; several large sawmills; desiccated coconut plants, the largest one employing about 2000 people; coconut oil mills and soap factories; rope and cordage firms; a huge pineapple cannery; and the large cigar factories. As compared with their prewar predecessors, many of these industries have shown significant progress and increased production by the use of new machinery or other improved techniques and procedures, by expanding the line of products manufactured, by more efficient use of by-products, by the entrance of more foreign capital, or as a result of better labor relations.

The third group consisted of a few sizable truly Philippine industries. Some of them were subsidized by the government through the National Development Corporation program, under which the

[1] Some of the following paragraphs are adapted from the author's "Industrial Progress in the Philippines," *Journal of Geography*, Vol. 55, 1956, pp. 131-136, and his "Industrialization in the Philippines," *Philippine Geographical Journal*, Vol. 6, 1958, pp. 8-17.

government absorbed some of the costs of production in the interests of national need. The large cement plant at Naga, Cebu, and two cotton textile plants are illustrative. Others in this group—including a large plant manufacturing American-type cigarettes, a paper mill, a large brewery, and a glass factory—represented private investment.

The paper mill at the Bais sugar central in Oriental Negros is a pioneer in the use of sugar-cane bagasse as a basic raw material in the manufacture of fine printing, bond, and typing papers on a commercial scale. It commanded the attention of paper-makers the world over. Several other paper plants (in India, Brazil, and the United States, for example) now use bagasse, following the pattern set by the Bais mill.

INDUSTRIAL GROWTH SINCE 1950

Each of these three major types of manufacturing plants has shown an increase in the past few years as a result in part of United States and United Nations technical assistance funds, but more so as a result of a new national impetus to industrial development—a national recognition that the Philippine economy is grossly overbalanced in favor of agriculture.

Major development of the past several years illustrates this emphasis upon industry. New plants produce hydroelectric power (discussed in Chapter 6), various steel products, refined petroleum, aluminum products, fertilizer, cement, rubber tires, zippers, drugs, jute and kraft paper bags, cotton and ramie textiles, foods, plastics, electronic equipment, paints, and flashlight batteries. Restrictions on the purchase of producers' goods abroad has slowed the pace of industrialization on occasion, but the trend is established. The Philippines is the most nearly industrialized country in Southeast Asia. More than 50 percent of the more than half million employed in non-agricultural industries work in manufacturing.

Steel and Shipyards. The Philippine steel industry is meager by Western standards. It is essentially various aspects of steel fabrication. There are a half-dozen steel rolling mills (most of them small), a shipyard, three plants making galvanized iron sheets, a nail factory, and plants making steel office furniture, zippers, and other miscellaneous items.

The original development plan of the National Steel and Shipbuilding Corporation (Nassco) included pig iron production, steel, rolling mills, and shipyards. At present Nassco is operating the Iligan Steel Mills and the Bataan National Shipyards, but according to the original plan these units should have been established only after Nassco had constructed an iron ore smelting plant. Since, at present, Nassco has no facilities for economical processing of iron ore into pig iron, the government decided to implement the second and third phases before concentrating on the problem of pig iron production. The steel mill, using Maria Cristina power, can be a profitable venture, but the shipyards need subsidization in some form. This weakness is fully recognized by the Philippine government, but it does not disturb Philippine economists, for the shipyards of the United States, the United Kingdom, and some other countries are subsidized, at least in part. The shipyards have completed only a few vessels, all small ones (1,600 ton capacity) for the interisland trade.

Fertilizer. A fertilizer plant is a near must in a country that is trying very hard to modernize its agriculture. This industry has been envisioned for many years, but without cheap power[2] it was not considered feasible. Initiated with United States Point Four funds (later MSA and FOA funds), it helps to provide fertilizer (ammonium sulphate) to the rice farmer and the sugar planter at a significantly lower cost than he must pay for imported fertilizer. The first plant (50,000 tons annual capacity) has now been supplemented by a second one of comparable size which uses local rather than imported raw materials.

Cement. There are now more than a half-dozen cement plants in the Philippines, some of them financed by the government and some by private capital. Whether each of them is properly located from the standpoint of the productive factors of the industry may be debatable. But the expansion of an industry that uses bulky raw materials and manufactures a heavy product is significant. Probably no modern industrial economy has attained that position without a significant domestic cement industry. Indeed, some geographers and

[2] The word "cheap" is used only in a relative sense. It is not cheap power by Western or Japanese standards.

economists believe that the cement industry of a country is the best single index to the industrial development of that country. Domestic cement plants now supply the normal demands of the construction industry and the highway paving program in the Philippines.

Aluminum. The new aluminum plant, in the Manila area, is the foil and sheet rolling mill of Reynolds Philippine Corporation. Owned jointly by a group of Philippine investors (49 percent) and by Reynolds Metals (51 percent), it began operations in May, 1955. Currently, imported aluminum pigs are melted and recast into slabs suitable for rolling. Long-range plans envision the eventual production of raw aluminum at or near Maria Cristina Falls. This venture of joint Philippine and foreign capital is illustrative of the method by which many of the newer industries are financed. It is a sound procedure, practiced in many countries where limited local capital and technical skills may handicap industrial progress.

Petroleum Refining. Much of the new industry represents the investment of private American capital in the Philippines. The first Philippine petroleum refinery (Caltex), on Batangas Bay, 60 miles from Manila, is representative. Initially a $15,000,000 refinery with a daily capacity of 13,000 barrels of crude oil, it now processes 30,000 barrels daily. Even so, it is not large in comparison with those in world-famous refinery areas. However, it was another important first in a country that had heretofore depended entirely upon the importation of refined petroleum products for its cars and trucks, mechanized farm equipment, Diesel power plants, interisland shipping, military and civilian aircraft, and Coleman lanterns. The land for the refinery, purchased in 1952, lies on the shore of spacious Batangas Bay and is a near-ideal site and position for a petroleum refinery. It began operations in 1955. Crude oil is purchased in Sumatra, and all manufactured products are marketed in the Philippines.

As proof of success, three other refineries have been built, also in the Manila region (Bataan, Cavite, and Batangas). The first two, operated by Standard Vacuum and Shell, are of 25,000 barrel capacity and, like the earlier one, are subsidiaries of foreign oil concerns, but with some Philippine capital invested. The third, Filoil, is smaller (10,000 barrels daily). It is primarily a Philippine venture into the industry, but some capital and technical leadership are supplied by a major American oil company, Gulf. All refineries follow the same general pattern of importing oil from the Indies and marketing their products in the Philippines, primarily by barge.

Philippine industrialization policy attaches no priority to manufacturing for export. It simply seeks to preserve domestic markets for domestic producers and to increase the variety of Philippine manufactures. Current expansion centers on *consumer goods*. This policy is sound for a country with limited fuel resources and a large domestic market. In 1951 there was one cotton textile mill; by late 1962 there were 25 in operation along with dozens of small garment factories of one type or another. Many of these plants are small, but some of them are modern structures on former paddy land on the outskirts of Manila. The newest and largest is one of five in the world using underground air-duct circulation. It employs 800 persons and makes denim, khaki, chambray, and other staple fabrics. Philippine production in 1961 was 370,000,000 yards of cloth. There are now two flour mills, both having started operations since 1958. One, in the Manila area, produces 50,000 tons yearly, and a larger one has just begun operation at Iligan, Mindanao. A modern glass factory making coke bottles, beer bottles, and other containers has been in operation since 1949, and a smaller plate-glass factory was started in 1959. There has been continued growth in processing of food products, particularly various preserves and fish products. Unfortunately, there is reason to believe that food processing has lagged behind other phases of industrial development. (Possibly this can be explained, in part, by the fact that although the Filipino has an Oriental environment and economy, he has developed a Western appetite. His processed foods, if he can afford them, tend to be imported, rather than domestic products.)

DOMINANCE OF THE MANILA
INDUSTRIAL DISTRICT

Manila has been, and still is, the industrial center of the country. But since 1950 industry has been moving to the suburbs. More specifically, new industrial construction is outside the political limits of crowded Manila—along the Pasig River in Quezon City or Pasay, in the Marikina Valley of Rizal, or in Cavite, Batangas, Bulacan, or even Bataan. A list of manufacturing firms in Manila proper, compiled by the Philippine Bureau of the Census in 1962, indicates that no significant industry has been established within Manila since 1958. The only sizable industrial complex apart from the Manila area is Iligan, Mindanao, where 16 manufacturing plants are in operation or under construction. Here, Maria Cristina power is the localizing factor. Although most of these plants are small, the Iligan area is fast becoming the most industrialized region outside of the Manila complex.

Two-fifths of the more than 11,000 Philippine manufacturing establishments with five or more employees are in the Manila area. According to Department of Labor figures these establishments employ more than half of the workers in industry and almost two-thirds of the women employed in industry. (By comparison, the province of Cebu has less than six percent of the country's industrial establishments.)

A great variety of factors contribute to this dominant position of Manila and its suburbs. Both the political center and the principal port, Manila is the focus of transportation lines and the banking and financial center of the country. There is a greater amount and variety of managerial talents and a ready supply of different types of skills in Manila. (In 1959 the Manila labor market area contained 10 percent of the Philippine population.) Because of the greater concentration of population and a higher purchasing power of much of that population, the Manila area is *the* prime market of the country.

The most important categories of manufacturing in the Manila industrial district are spinning, weaving, and the production of wearing apparel; food and beverage processing; and the base metals, metal-working, and machinery group. These three segments account for two-thirds of the employees in Manila manufacturing plants. The new petroleum refineries are too far from the city to be an integral part of the Manila industrial complex or to be considered within the Manila labor market area.

The percentage of women employees in industry is higher in Manila than in other parts of the country, almost 20 percent of the total. This proportion is a logical reflection of the importance in the Manila area of those industry groups that provide a greater opportunity for feminine employment—textiles and wearing apparel, food and beverages, and tobacco products. In the Philippines 61 percent of the employees in tobacco manufactures are women. Workers in textile mills and apparel factories are 37 percent women; in the foods and beverage group, 14 percent.

Outside of the Manila area most manufacturing is non-durable or consumer goods. The foods and beverages group is generally the principal one. In Cebu Province this group accounts for one-third of the total. In Negros Occidental, sugar *centrals* dominate the industrial scene. Batangas manufacturing includes textiles and wearing apparel, coconut products, and petroleum products.

IMPETUS TO MANUFACTURING

The largest single inducement to Philippine industrial growth was provided by import controls. This protective measure offset, to some extent, the prevalent aversion to risking capital in anything except real estate and commercial ventures. (During 1950, the year that import control and foreign-exchange restriction was imposed, 164 manufacturing firms were formed.) Unfortunately, some of the new manufacturing concerns in the early 1950's were merely a means of exercising import privileges for raw materials, which instead of being further fabricated in the usual sense were sold immediately on the market with only token alteration or modification. Moreover, some of these Filipino corporations are essentially partnerships. The use of a corporation to expand outside ownership and secure new capital was a rare exception in 1950. Despite these negative aspects, the over-all impact was favorable. Domestic capital has become less timid, and some of the more recent expansion has been with foreign capital. In the final analysis Philippine industrialization has been aggressively promoted by public policies and governmental actions, including subsidization of market institutions and protection from outside competition.

HANDICAPS TO INDUSTRIALIZATION

Industralization in the Philippines faces several major difficulties. The first is the near-poverty of the majority of the population, which handicaps the successful operation of industry. The reason is clear: if only a small proportion of the people have enough income to purchase a commodity, the market for that product is definitely limited.

A second handicap to industrialization is the generally inadequate development of transportation facilities. In an insular country an integration of rail facilities is difficult, if not impossible. The only important railroad, in Luzon, is a single line that must compete with water transportation because the shape of the island causes coastwise traffic to more or less parallel the railroad. Truck traffic is slow and costly. It may appear that the national and provincial highways permit access to all parts of the country, but most of them are coastal highways that do not adequately serve interior settlements. Moreover, paved highways are limited to parts of Luzon and the immediate environs of a half dozen or so of the principal cities in the southern islands. Interisland shipping lacks regulation. The number of vessels may be adequate, but since they were not designed for interisland traffic, the labor cost in handling a given cargo is greater than would otherwise be the case. In the absence of a maritime commission or other realistic regulating agency, the interisland fleet is operating at something less than peak efficiency.

A third handicap to industrial progress has been the attitude of many people with money for investment. In a pre-industrial society prestige is gained by ownership of land. To invest surplus funds for purposes of increasing production or of lowering cost has not been the normal Philippine way of using those funds. Although this attitude is changing, substantial industrial growth must, for many years to come, depend to a considerable degree upon foreign investment. Under present world conditions this means chiefly investment from the United States, to a lesser extent from Western Europe and Japan. Only in these areas is there any appreciable number of concerns or individuals that are willing to risk investments abroad for the sake of the large potential returns that they may bring.

The fourth major handicap is the prevalence of a concept of national self-sufficiency. If industry can produce a given commodity at a low cost, the welfare of the people is thereby increased. But low-cost production is possible only when large quantities of goods are produced and when the raw materials are brought cheaply to the manufacturing plant. If a country insists that it make use of its own raw materials even at high costs, or if a country insists that it must have its own basic steel industry as a foundation for industrialization, the people of that country may derive no real benefits from industrial progress. To use government subsidies to foster and protect a steel industry based largely or entirely upon imported raw materials increases production costs and may eventually result in economic disaster. (Japan does have a steel industry that is based largely upon imported raw materials, but this handicap is offset by extremely cheap labor and a large domestic market. Probably no other country can duplicate this combination of circumstances.) There are two alternatives: to accept international dependence and give up the concept of national self-sufficiency, as Switzerland and Japan have done; or to accept the thesis that all labor is for the benefit of the state and accept high-cost products.

Philippine labor is a fifth handicap to rapid industrial development, despite the fact that there is an adequate labor force which seeks employment. It is not an illiterate labor force, and it is not expensive in terms of hourly or daily wages. However, the total labor cost in terms of individual productivity is high. If and when Philippine labor becomes an efficient producer over a long period of time, Philippine industry may expand very rapidly.

THE OUTLOOK FOR INDUSTRIALIZATION

Philippine manufacturing has grown from an insignificant activity before World War II to the modest beginning of an industrialized society. The most rapidly growing sector of the national economy, it now accounts for about one-fifth of the national income, as compared with one-twelfth before 1950. It reflects natural endowments, social trends, political conflicts, and economic ideologies. It pervades the national psychology. Progress is real and meaningful, but Philippine manufacturing is costly.

The Philippines will probably never become a Britain or a Japan, but there is reason to believe that industrial progress can continue at a moderate pace. To accurately estimate the industrial potential and to recommend areas of worthwhile expansion may require a more penetrating study of Philippine geography in relation to large-scale industry than has yet appeared. The productive factors have not been adequately evaluated in terms of the Philippine environment.

Philippine leaders are only now becoming realistic with respect to a manufacturing economy. They are beginning to recognize that:

(1) Economic self-sufficiency is a dream. Capital follows trade. Even large countries with varied resources (such as the United States, the U.S.S.R., Canada, and Brazil) are not economically independent.

(2) The myth that foreign capital leads to economic domination is without foundation. European capital built United States railroads and developed its mines and factories long before that country was a great power. Canada and Australia have experienced great economic prosperity during the past decade, but have attained this position, to a large extent, with the aid of foreign capital.

(3) Economic development does not necessarily mean a high degree of industrialization. Denmark and the Netherlands are basically agricultural countries, yet each of them has a highly-developed economy. Successful industrialization must be geared to the people's capacity to absorb industrialization. Otherwise, the economy will collapse. A balanced agro-industrial economy is a sound economy.

(4) There is no case in recorded history to indicate that an industrial economy can be formulated by legislation or administrative decree. Import controls can be defended as a temporary measure. They provided an initial stimulus to Philippine manufacturing that could not have been provided by any other means at the time they were placed in effect. But they are indefensible as a long-range plan to develop an industrial society. President Macapagal's action to

free the country's economy from some of the now-unrealistic controls (January 21, 1962) is commendable.

Potentially, the Philippines is in a reasonably strong position with respect to industrial development—in fact, in a stronger position than most of its neighbors. Probably no country of comparable size has as great a variety of mineral wealth. Among the basic raw materials of modern industry, only good quality coal is lacking. There is relative economic stability. In Monsoon Asia, the Philippine per capita income is surpassed only by Japan and Malaysia, which should make possible a moderately high ratio of savings and investment without sacrificing educational and health standards. The population has a relatively high level of literacy, more than three-fourths of the people can read and write, and the ratio between population and resources is still small. Together, these factors provide a strong basis for the development of a sound economy based upon a balance between agriculture, manufacturing, and the extractive industries. Can the government and the people provide the continued mature leadership that is necessary? Can the labor force rise to the challenge before it is too late?

8   *Philippine Commercial Centers, Transportation, and Commerce*

M OST states have developed by a process of accretion around a nuclear core that has fostered integration and nationhood. In most countries this core is the most populous part of the nation, tends to remain constant, and contains the central organs of development. The Paris Basin has formed the heart of France; the Lower Nile has been a lifeline across Egypt; and the Kwanto (Tokyo) Plain has long been the most important segment of Japan. As a nation develops, lines of transport penetrate beyond the basic nucleus. In European countries the capital cities are the primary centers, and transportation lines radiate from them as the spokes of a wheel radiate from the axle. Thereby the hinterland is tied to the core area. In the American colonies the original centers along the Atlantic seaboard were initially a series of nuclear cores from which a large, modern country developed. Chicago and Detroit became major cities only after the development of a transportation net had tied them to the eastern centers and to each other. Hence, the growth of transportation and other forms of communication make it possible to develop the component parts of the state that lie beyond the nucleus. A type of cohesion evolves, and regional centers become important secondary nuclei. In each of the Southeast Asian countries a dominant city has developed. Regional centers are in the process of evolution.

THE PHILIPPINE CORE AREA

The core area of the Philippines is the Central Plain of Luzon, that elongated lowland of about 150 by 40 miles that extends from Lingayan Gulf on the north to Tayabas Bay on the south. The southern part of the Central Plain is the heart of the Philippine Tagalog area, and Tagalog is the basis of the designated national language. Metropolitan Manila is the focal point or nucleus of this core. The functional capital and largest city of the country, Manila is also the financial center and the transportation hub of the Republic. It is the center of the airline net, the headquarters of the principal railroad, and the home port of much of the interisland shipping. Several paved roads lead from it, and highway traffic justifies a circumferential road around it. Manila is the educational center and the religious center as well. Its newspapers are read throughout the country. As a world port and the gateway to the Western urban world, Manila is a primate city and a heavily commercialized one. Probably its most important single function is that of distribution. By value, the foreign trade of Manila surpasses that of all other Philippine ports of entry combined. Finally, Manila and its suburbs contain most of the manufacturing plants. With a population approaching two million, metropolitan Manila is truly a national center. There is prestige to work or study in Manila, to be from Manila, to have business to take one to Manila.

REGIONAL CENTERS

Including Manila, five interregional trade centers have been delimited by Ullman.[1] By comparison with the national capital, the other four are small. They resemble regional market towns or small wholesale centers of the United States, but each of them functions as a local *entrepôt,* particularly for the export of at least one of the major raw materials of foreign trade. All of them have reasonably satisfactory hotel facilities. Except for Zamboanga, each center has two or more colleges or universities.

Cebu City (205,000 in 1959) is the second city of the Philippines both in population and as a commercial center. It serves an area having about 25 percent of the nation's population. Because it is more centrally located than Manila and has a large water hinterland, its domestic shipping is slightly greater than that of the national center. Air passenger traffic is heavy, but land trade is meager. Cebu

[1] Edward L. Ullman, "Trade Centers and Tributary Areas in the Philippines," *Geographical Review,* Vol. 50, 1960, pp. 203-218.

City functions as a regional *entrepôt,* concerning itself primarily with collecting, handling, sorting, grading, processing, breaking bulk, and reshipping.[2] It is the leading center for the export of copra.

Iloilo (125,000), on Panay, divides the central Philippine area with Cebu and the western Visayan area with Bacolod, which is approaching interregional status. Formerly the major sugar port, Iloilo has failed to keep pace with the other centers in the postwar years, largely because sugar is now loaded directly from lighters to offshore ships anchored opposite the Negros centrals. At the same time Bacolod has become a distribution center of increasing magnitude, particularly for machinery, equipment, and other agricultural supplies.

Davao (60,000) in southeastern Mindanao, although isolated in one corner of the country, has road and water connections to surrounding areas and is an interregional center of increasing magnitude. Originally noted primarily for the export of abaca, and secondly for shipment of copra, it has assumed somewhat more diversified service functions within the past decade. Its importance is attested, in part, by the fact that there are daily direct air flights to and from Manila as well as flights with scheduled intermediate stops. Although handicapped by its peripheral position, Davao is a terminal center with a significant tributary area of growing economic importance.

Zamboanga (25,000) in southwestern Mindanao is the smallest and probably the weakest of the interregional centers. Its hinterland, consisting of parts of western and southern Mindanao and the Sulu Islands, is served largely by water transportation. Primarily copra and some abaca are exported from Zamboanga, and logs and lumber are shipped from nearby production sites that are within the Zamboanga Customs District. Foreign ships call at Zamboanga in large numbers, but it is more important as an interisland port, probably ranking third among them in amount of domestic commerce.

Next in order of magnitude are more than 30 major regional centers, the regional market towns of the Philippines. Most of them are coastal communities with good interisland service, and at some

[2] Fred L. Wernstedt, "Cebu: Focus of Interisland Trade," *Economic Geography,* Vol. 32, 1956, pp. 336-346.

of them ocean vessels load and discharge cargo. About half of them have an airfield with at least biweekly service. Nearly all of them are provincial capitals with some political influence at the regional level. Capital cities normally are the site of the provincial high school and in some cases a trade school as well. A few have a private college or a provincial normal college. With one or two exceptions each has a cathedral and a secondary school operated by the Catholic Church. Most also have a provincial hospital. They are regional centers of a secondary order comparable to a large Midwestern county seat and retail center. They furnish the basic urban service of an indefinite and irregular area and provide a wide range of economic, political and social services.

TRANSPORTATION

Railway, highway, airway, and water transportation are important in the Philippines. The development and present status of each tends to reflect the geographical, historical, political, economic, and cultural forces of varying local and national significance. Primarily because of the scattered-island character of the Philippine Archipelago and the absence of sizable plains areas even on the larger islands, a truly efficient and economical means of domestic transportation is yet to be developed. This is a crucial requisite of a modern state; its need is readily apparent.

A striking characteristic of Philippine transportation systems, compared with those of the Western world, is the co-existence of primitive and modern means of transport. Both may share the same facility. Each may form an individual cog in the flow of goods and the movement of people. Zamboanga harbor presents an exotic transportation landscape. It may be used simultaneously by a large international cargo carrier of foreign registry, the crowded general-purpose interisland vessel, the local ferry to Basilan, the picturesque Moro *vinta* (an elaborate dugout canoe with outriggers) and the outrigger canoe of the "Sea Gypsy" who comes alongside to sell shells or coral. Only slightly less colorful is the traffic on a paved modern highway in rural Luzon where a few automobiles, trucks, jeeps, and rural buses share the highway with bullock or carabao carts and pedestrians. Abaca, grown as a cash crop in the hills of southern Negros, must be carried on the backs of men along footpaths to roadhead, then hauled by truck to Dumaguete for shipment to processing plant or for export. This utilization of a combination of transport systems to permit a non-perishable commodity to reach its market is duplicated with slight variations in frontier Mindanao, Palawan, Mindoro, the mountains of Luzon, and elsewhere.

WATER COMMERCE

The Philippines is a maritime country. Historically, the movement of people and products was along the coastlines and between the islands. Some culture groups were truly seafaring people and often sailed considerable distances to trade. More representative, however, was the movement over shorter distances and along wellknown neighboring coasts. Nonetheless, the economy has always been based upon maritime commerce, whether it be local, interisland, or international. Fourteen domestic and 37 international shipping lines now serve the country. There are some 350 public ports, of which 25 are ports of entry for ships engaged in foreign trade.

Throughout all stages of modern Philippine history, *interisland shipping* has maintained a position of dominance. In all, there are more than 60 active interisland ports (seven of them are also international ports). Most of them are population centers; many of them are provincial capitals. They are, then, the cultural, economic, and political foci of the many local areas that they serve.

Growth has not been consistent and uniform. From a modest beginning with primitive sailing craft, the Spaniards added small steamers that meandered among the islands. From this seeming lack of organization and integration emerged a few companies with scheduled operations. Although vessels were small and speeds were slow, the shipping routes in 1898 were not unlike those of today. An elementary pattern had emerged. But for a combination of reasons, domestic commerce virtually ceased during the period of Spanish-American conflict and the years immediately following. After it was reestablished with United States Coast Guard vessels, route contracts were awarded to private companies where trade was sufficient to attract non-government shipping. Still later, interisland shipping was left to its own initiative under loose governmental supervision and control.[3]

By 1940 some 15 companies were employed in interisland and coastwise shipping, and approximately 1,800 steam, diesel, and larger sailing vessels operated over interisland routes. Probably almost that many other registered vessels were involved in limited routes, a local coastwide traffic that was basically intraisland rather than interisland by definition. It is apparent, then, that the network of domestic shipping routes developed by the late 1930's included all parts of the Philippine island-world and that the fleet included the most varied types of ships, from small outrigger canoes to 5,000-ton vessels. The fleet was adequate to meet all normal demands. Some of the vessels had been designed and constructed especially for this interisland service and had good passenger accommodations.

The Pacific War brought an abrupt end to interisland shipping. Virtually the entire fleet was destroyed. At the end of the war the situation was critical. A rapid rehabilitation was essential, and it was possible only because vessels were made available by the United States Maritime Commission and the American Navy. This procedure resulted in a hodge-podge of craft, none of them designed for interisland cargo and passenger traffic, but the crisis was alleviated. Some of these emergency vessels are still in operation.

Generally speaking, the shipping industry made a rapid and successful recovery, but it still lacks positive direction, and cargo costs remain high. It can be characterized as scheduled between major interisland ports, but sporadic to minor ports along the shipping lanes, the latter being dependent upon availability of cargo. The Bureau of Customs of the Philippine Republic exercises jurisdiction over interisland shipping, but maintenance of standards, regulation, supervision, and control are very nominal. In the lack of a realistic maritime code lies one of the real needs of the Philippines today.

Some 7,000 vessels are now engaged actively in interisland commerce. Most of the powered vessels are war surplus ships acquired from the United States Government. Wernstedt groups them into

[3] Fred L. Wernstedt, *The Role and Importance of Philippine Interisland Shipping,* Office of Naval Research, Contract number Nonr 656 (08), page 11 ff.

six categories based upon their normal use. Five of them contribute to interisland trade; the sixth is intraisland in character. They are:

(1) The interisland core fleet, which through its regularly scheduled, multi-ports-of-call operations provides the basic framework of the domestic commerce;

(2) The feeder or commuting fleet, which functions to supplement the core-fleet operations, normally by providing connections between off-route ports and ports served by the core fleet;

(3) Special-purpose cargo vessels, more often company owned (or company leased), which function to supply bulk transport for petroleum, minerals, and lumber;

(4) Barges and lighters;

(5) Commercial fishing vessels; and

(6) A vast number of smaller vessels not obviously engaged in any but the most local commercial operations.[4]

Coastwise shipping utilizes many different types of vessels—surplus landing craft, barges, launches and motorboats, dugouts powered by outboard motors, and sailboats of varying descriptions. This is a local transit service that is multifunctional and non-scheduled, except around the principal ports and between sizable coastal towns where no road parallels the coast. It may be the only service among small contiguous islands and between them and the principal port that serves them. It may serve essentially to collect products for export—copra, for example. It may be primarily a passenger and package cargo service, operated by retail or wholesale merchants and originally designed to distribute imported commodities. More likely it will carry whatever is to be hauled, whether it be agricultural raw materials, cans or drums of petroleum products, rice or corn, beer or Coca-Cola, imported products, people, poultry, or possibly livestock. It probably provides a local mail and message service, as well.

River transportation, too, supplements and complements the interisland service. Twenty-two rivers are listed as navigable for craft drawing three feet. Most of them are small and navigable only for short distances; in fact, except for a few larger streams on Luzon and Mindanao, the transportation value of the rivers is almost nil. Within a local area or even on an inter-village level, however, rivers

[4] *Ibid.,* p. 19.

are still valuable as a means of local transit by banca. This is especially true during the wet season when roads and trails may be flooded or otherwise difficult to use. Local transportation by banca occurs at any season where there is an extended net of inland waters, for example, on the margins of the Pampanga Delta of Luzon where the lower reaches of the river have divided into many channels.

The present network of roads in the Philippines, and the extension of bus and truck feeder lines to the railway system, has served to negate the former importance of river traffic, except in a few cases. Export products, principally logs and lumber, are still moved by water on the Agusan in Mindanao. The Pasig, which meanders through Manila into Manila Bay, remains important for barge traffic used to transport heavy cargos, such as sand, cement, steel, petroleum products, and copra. Limited barge traffic remains on the lower Cagayan (Luzon) and some of the rivers of Negros and Mindanao. And on many rivers, both large and small, bamboo may be floated downstream.

RAILWAY TRANSPORT

The history of Philippine railroads begins in 1894 when an English corporation under a government franchise completed a line (3 foot, 6 inch gauge) from Manila to Dagupan on Lingayan Gulf. This is the present route of the northern extension of the Manila Railroad Company, which was subsequently extended southeast from Manila to Legaspi and Tabaco. The American-owned Philippine Railroad built lines on Cebu (1909) and Panay. There are a few minor branches, really spurs, but essentially these are single lines, rather than a rail net in the Western sense. Finally, there are more than a dozen narrow-gauge, private, industrial systems operated by sugar centrals or lumber mills. Most of these private lines are of lightweight 30-inch gauge and are not interconnected with public carriers. However, the individual systems on western Negros are interconnected with neighboring systems to provide a workable emergency net throughout the sugar-producing area of Occidental Negros. The small locomotives on them use bagasse or alcohol for fuel.

The railroads suffered heavily as a result of World War II. Bridges were destroyed; rolling stock was lost or left to rust; cross-ties had been removed; and the roadbeds were left in poor condition. Immediately following the war, even with the United States assistance received, there were insufficient locomotives and rolling stock. The Cebu line was not rebuilt. Instead, its equipment and rails were cannabalized to put the Panay line into operation.

The Manila Railroad, government owned since 1917, has shown the greatest modernization. The first air-conditioned passenger car was acquired in 1950, the first diesel locomotive shortly later. The line is now completely dieselized with Japanese equipment. Imported bunker oil was used originally, but the new petroleum refineries should make it no longer necessary to rely upon imported fuel.

The only likely expansion of rail facilities (now about 600 miles) is that of the heavily subsidized Manila Railroad, and this possible expansion appears to be limited. Private bus lines have cut tremendously into railroad passenger traffic. Bus fares are cheaper; moreover, service is more frequent and more convenient, for buses often provide a kind of door-to-door service. Cargo traffic by truck has also increased at the expense of the railroad. The farm-to-warehouse, mine-to-port, or door-to-door service is more desirable, and truck service is normally faster than rail service. Most of the new factories are without rail service.

HIGHWAY TRANSPORT

The earlier concentrations of population were along the coast and along the rivers because water transportation provided easy access. With the introduction of the motor vehicle and the development of roads, there has been a change in attitude and the way of life in the rural Philippines. A reorientation of settlement pattern has occurred. Families that lived in relative isolation have moved to the shoulders of the highway and aligned themselves along it. Where the highway parallels the coast, new houses face the roadway rather than the sea. The construction of new highways in frontier areas has been stressed in the postwar years. New settlements have mushroomed along them, and in some cases older barrios have moved to them. Whatever the history, most smaller communities wherever roads have been constructed are characterized by a shoestring form with dwelling units aligned along a road of some kind—that is, the linear dimension of the settlement is considerably greater than its width. So highway traffic provides essentially a front-door service.

There is a reasonably good highway net on much of Luzon and in parts of the Visayas—the Panay Plain and northwestern Negros, for example. New highways have been built into interior Mindanao so that a skeleton net exists. But there are few roads in the mountainous areas on any of the islands. Palawan, Western Mindoro, parts of Samar, and segments of the east coast of Luzon and Mindanao are still dependent primarily on water transport and occasional air service. There is often a single road along a segment of coast, possibly with a secondary road or roads that extend upstream along a river valley and penetrate into the interior hills or mountains for a short distance. Most Philippine roads are surfaced with sand, gravel, or crushed coralline limestone. Frontier roads and spurs from paved highways into the adjacent foothills or mountains may be only graded earthen roads, often badly in need of repair. Yet, by Asian standards Philippine roads are good. Rural highways are wider than the roads of rural Japan. The highway net is superior to that of other Southeast Asian countries. In Asia, probably only Japan and India have a greater mileage of paved highways.

Paved highways in the Philippines are built upon firm roadbeds with wide shoulders. It is possible to travel from Manila to Laoag in the far northwest or to Legaspi on the southeast coast of Luzon on concrete or good "black-top." Equally good spurs extend from this highway to Baguio, to Cabanatuan and San Jose, to Batangas, and to other secondary centers. In the Visayas and Mindanao paved highways are limited to short stretches that extend along the coast from some of the principal ports. The longest paved highway outside of Luzon is along the western and northern coast of Negros. Traffic flow counts indicate that daily vehicular traffic is heavy in Manila and nearby areas of Luzon, around Cebu City, and from Bacolod northward on Negros; moderately heavy in the central Cagayan Valley and around Baguio, Iloilo, Davao, and a few other centers; generally light elsewhere. For 60,000 or more passenger cars and a slightly larger number of commercial vehicles there are a little more than 22,000 miles of highways of all classes. Probably half this amount can be designated as first-class roads, but outside the cities not more than 1,000 miles is modern paved highway.

Except in a few cities and nearby areas, highway traffic includes more buses and trucks—and possibly more jeeps and jeepneys—than motor cars. Most of the trucks are owned by mining companies, lumber mills, coconut processing plants, rice mills, stevedoring companies, or other concerns that operate them as a part of their normal business operation. There is only a very nominal number of trucks for public hire, and only a few of the larger farming operations can afford and use a truck or trucks.

Most Philippine buses consist of a locally constructed body built upon an imported truck chassis. Urban buses are passenger carriers with individual fixed seats on either side of a center isle. Standard rural buses have wooden benches extending the width of the bus and with entrance only from the right side of the vehicle. Cargo space is generally provided between the wheels along each side. This is the usual location for hauling bags of rice, cases of Coca-Cola, cartons of canned milk, crates of chickens, and a variety of other cargo, probably at no additional cost to its passenger-owner. Rear "seats" are removable to provide additional cargo space if the occasion warrants.

The ubiquitous jeepney is a Philippine institution that reflects an astounding display of ingenuity. In part because of the paucity of public transportation immediately after the war, the war-surplus army jeep was converted by the hundreds into passenger vehicles to carry 6, 8, or 12 persons. A canvas canopy covers the entire body, sometimes with a fringe on top. Drab army and navy colors were covered by assorted brighter hues, and equally colorful names were painted upon the side (*Rose Marie, Pasay Flyer, The Atom Bomb, I Will Return*). Normally required to follow designated routes or streets, the jeepney provides a service that is as cheap as the local bus but faster. As the original vehicles required replacement, new jeep chassis were imported for immediate adaptation to the expanding jeepney fleet. Most of them are owner operated; a new entrepreneur has entered the transportation scene. In many cases the

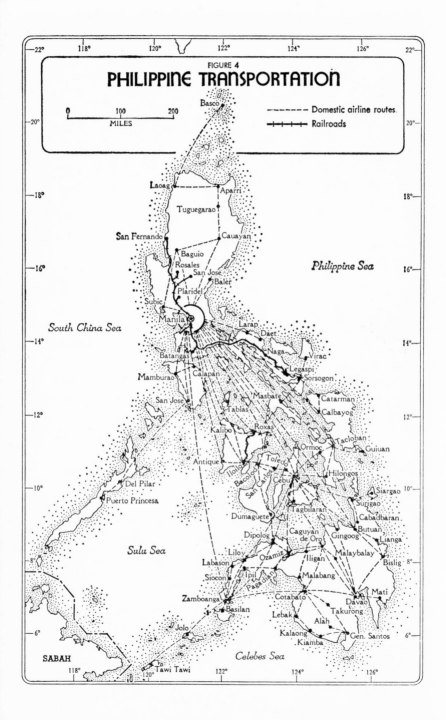

FIGURE 4

PHILIPPINE TRANSPORTATION

0   100   200
MILES

------- Domestic airline routes.
+++++ Railroads

single operator with his single vehicle has become the primary source of income for his family.

In a practical sense the jeepney has replaced the prewar horse-drawn *calesa* and *carretella*. Used primarily for urban passenger service, jeepneys are found in virtually every province, but most of them are in Manila and its suburbs. Nonetheless, they are an important service in many provincial communities and may give somewhat regular service from a regional or secondary center to nearby barrios. On occasion, they may be hired for a specific trip, thus competing with the taxi or providing taxi service where no taxis are available, as from some provincial airports into town.

AIRWAYS

Philippine Airlines provides an extremely efficient service to about 40 domestic airports and connects the principal islands and most distant provinces with Manila. (See Figure 4.) The government is the principal owner, but the line is managed by the minority stockholders, Andres Soriano and Company. In contrast with the generally tardy and often unscheduled rail, highway, and water transportation, air service is frequent, and exact schedules are maintained. For businessmen the air service has proven extremely valuable. Manila is the hub of air transport, but Cebu and Cagayan de Oro are secondary centers from which flights radiate in the Visayas and Mindanao respectively. Logically, air transportation is greater in interisland communication than between points that can be reached by land routes. Air mail is important, and Manila newspapers are distributed by air. There are a few daily scheduled cargo flights. Spare parts and pharmaceuticals are distributed from the capital city by air. On occasion, chickens, fish, and vegetables are flown from the Visayas and Mindanao to Manila.

Nine international airlines use the Manila International Airport and make it an important link in the communications of eastern and southern Asia as well as a point of departure for some trans-Pacific flights. Philippine Airlines ceased its international flights to Europe and America in 1954 as an economy measure, but continued its Hong Kong schedule. In 1962 trans-Pacific flights were resumed and the Hong Kong schedule was extended to Bangkok.

Insularity causes geographic fragmentation of the national domain and creates difficulties in Philippine communication. The climatic regions differ markedly. Contrasts in economic interests are readily discernible. Racial and religious minorities create local friction. Linguistic problems are numerous. There is regionalism in Philippine agriculture and in national politics. Yet, despite these and other elements that contribute to a lack of uniformity, the impressive thing about the Filipinos is their unity, not their diversity.

PHILIPPINE NATIONALISM

Immediately after the Pacific War nationalism blossomed to flower throughout Southeast Asia, but in every country the seeds from which it sprouted had been planted long years before. It evolved over a long period from a combination of historical events. In each country it was the result of many interrelated, complex forces in the cultural matrix of the area. Although the principle of nationalism is a Western concept, in the countries of Southeast Asia its strongest expression was in a widespread movement against a Western colonial regime. Only the date and national circumstances differ from country to country.

Nationalism was inappropriate to the traditional society of the Philippines. There was little to bridge the gap between the ruling landholders and commercial groups who worked the land. Then, unity against Spain created a consciousness of solidarity. America encouraged the development of a national pride. Local forces exerted great counter-pressures, but the fight against Japan removed any remaining tendency toward separatism. Filipinos take pride in their history, its heroes, and its martyrs. The symbolic Juan de la Cruz (Mr. Average Citizen) has a strong pride in his local origin, but he is first a Filipino; only second is he a Bikolano, or a Cebuano, or an Ilokano. The people are proud of their independence, of the fact that they have "the best democracy in Asia," and of their country's role in regional and world affairs. National fervor is high. There is a strong Philippine national pride.

Nationalism in Asia wears strange guises, and Philippine nationalism has its distinctive character. There is a broad feeling of solidarity, but in recent years it has tended to have strong negative rather than positive aspects. A heightened love of and a militant stand on behalf of country has been overshadowed by a stressed need for economic independence. In practice, it has become economic nationalism, exemplified in federal policies with regard to exploitation of minerals, certain limitations to investment of foreign capital, and a strong emphasis on industrialization. It has meant a reduced influence of foreign firms and a stronger Filipinization of the economy.

Actually, economic nationalism roots deep in Philippine economic history. Violence directed toward the Chinese community persisted throughout the Spanish colonial period. Dependence upon, and inability to compete with, Chinese commercial and financial interests undoubtedly contributed much toward this feeling. Some animosity toward the extensive landholdings of Catholic missionary orders and individuals, both Spanish and American, helped to further this feeling, although to a markedly lesser extent. Economic nationalism, then, was a moderate and gradual movement, vastly subordinate to the desire for independence or political nationalism. It surged to the front only after independence became a reality, when the government was charged with the responsibility to promote national economic development.

Filipinization tended to occupy the Constitutional Convention behind the scenes and in discussion, even though the constitution itself is moderate in this respect. It can best be described as a somewhat obscured policy of de-alienization. Without specifically naming any particular group, it is aimed toward limitation of Chinese domination of industry and commerce. Filipinization encourages an expansion of Philippine economic activity relative to the normal expansion in alien participation; discourages, and in some cases prohibits, further growth in alien ownership; and establishes incentives for alien owners to divest themselves of their ownership. There has been no large-scale appropriation of foreign holdings by the state solely for redistribution to Philippine nationals, although property of deported non-resident aliens has been reassigned in this fashion in some instances. Government monopolization of foreign exchange has been used as an effective device to increase the Filipinos' share of import and retail trade. The exchange controls, be ginning in 1950, were designed as a means of currency control and to avoid great devaluation of the peso. As administered, the alien importer has been at a distinct disadvantage because requests for "dollar allocations" are not, and probably cannot be, evaluated in a totally objective atmosphere. In some cases, government monopolies established to implement exchange controls and to produce government revenues have nationalized export industries formerly dominated by aliens.[1]

In some segments of Philippine economy the American is not yet an alien. As an illustration, the Commonwealth Constitution provided that lands of the public domain containing minerals or forests were to remain the property of the state. These lands could be leased for periods not to exceed 25 years, but all such leases must be granted to citizens of the Philippines or to corporations that were of 60 percent Filipino ownership. Appended to the Constitution was a provision that citizens of the United States were to be granted the same rights as Filipinos to develop natural resources until the Philippines were granted independence. This same provision was extended to 1977 as a result of a 1948 agreement with the United States. Herein lies the basis for the large American investment and active participation in the Philippine mining and lumber industries.

The controlled economy that began in 1950 has been modified markedly. Three weeks after President Macapagal assumed office in 1962 he cancelled the restriction on foreign exchange and freed the peso from what had become unrealistic controls. Formerly pegged at two to the American dollar, it is now almost four (3.90

[1] For a detailed discussion of economic nationalism in the Philippines and its various ramifications see Frank H. Golay, *The Philippines: Public Policy and National Economic Development*, pp. 312-345.

in February, 1964) to the dollar. It is no longer necessary for private business to bribe officials in order to obtain exchange and import licences.

On the international scene, Filipino pride and its attendant national policy for economic independence does not resolve itself into blind or dogmatic opposition to the United States and to the West. Quite the contrary, Philippine national policy basically sides with the United States in the world struggle. Furthermore, Filipinos are akin to the United States in their fundamental belief in political democracy. The two ideological strains, nationalism and political democracy, are combined.

GOVERNMENTAL OPERATION

The Philippine Republic is governed under a constitution adopted May 14, 1935, when a plebiscite approved the United States plan of granting independence after a 10-year transitional period. There is a close similarity between it and the constitution of the United States, logically so because approval of the United States Congress was as necessary as was a favorable vote in the Philippine National Assembly and the subsequent approval of the people. The Philippine president is elected for four years and is eligible for election to a second term. There is a cabinet of 10 department heads to assist the president. The Philippine Congress is bicameral, the two houses bearing the same names (Senate and House of Representatives) as their American counterparts. There is a Supreme Court with a chief justice and 10 associate justices, a court of appeal, and a court for industrial relations. The Supreme Court, although more involved in political matters than its American model, is highly respected, probably because it is one of the few non-political institutions in the Philippine government.

The Philippine presidency, with powers and duties patterned after those of the United States chief executive, is a more powerful office in relation to other branches of the government than is the American presidency. "Item veto authority" over money and tariff bills is illustrative of this greater power vested in one man. Furthermore, the political power of the president is greater, relatively, because there is a higher percentage of appointive offices in the Philippine government than in American governmental organization. Filipino presidents have been subjected to severe criticism, no doubt much of it justified, but in each case they have been able to direct the executive organs of the state in a constitutional manner. They have held the country together through years of social and economic stress. The Philippine president and his congress have not always agreed. They have sometimes appeared to work at cross purposes, but they have worked for a common goal, in the determination of policy for the over-all welfare of the country. Law and order in the Philippines is superior to that of other newly independent lands in Southeast Asia. The strong hand of the presidency has contributed to a notable record of continuity and performance in its governmental institutions. In no sense is the Philippine Congress a rubber stamp, but the president is the power that runs the country.

THE ARMED FORCES

The armed services of the Philippines are not a political force in national affairs. The Philippine constabulary, before its merger with the army, was politically controlled, but the army has never been a prop of any political regime. The 50,000-man Philippine armed forces was the major factor in the defeat of the Communist Huk rebels, and Magsaysay used these actions as a springboard to the presidency. But he and other presidents, as well as Philippine military leaders, have regarded the primary role of the military as international in character. Its role in the control of internal peace and security is considered a necessary but secondary adjunct to the primary function—the fulfillment of Philippine Treaty commitments under the SEATO alliances and under the bilateral defense arrangements with the United States. The dispatch of an initial force of 1000 officers and men to Korea in late 1950, when the Huks were at the height of their terror raids and forces were therefore badly needed at home, may be attributed to national pride or international window dressing. But it is a representative illustration of national policy with respect to the function of the armed forces.

The Philippine armed forces, then, have been concerned with security, both internal and international. The military has never encroached noticeably on the economy or other segments of Philippine life and society. This policy is in marked contrast to Burma, where the army grows sugar cane, sells fish, breeds poultry, and operates a department store; where it ran the government for a period of two years beginning in July, 1958. It is distinctly different from Thailand, where the army dominates transportation and other phases of national life. It varies greatly from Indonesia, where the army has been used solely to preserve and restore internal security, where it has been and still is absolutely necessary for the survival of the nation and therefore has become a part of the stresses and strains of postcolonial politics. The Philippine army is charged with the preservation of law and order on election day, but it does not run the elections and does not count the votes. It may not be completely free of politics, but it is not a political force and is not likely to become a political institution.

LAW AND ORDER

Law enforcement traditionally has been a problem in some areas. Immediately following the Pacific war petty larceny was rampant in the Manila region, probably a natural consequence of the scarcity of goods and the difficulty of survival during the Japanese occupation. Banditry has occurred in Cavite sporadically throughout modern Philippine history. The former head hunters in the mountains of northern Luzon have made headlines, but fears have been grossly overemphasized. With normal precautions and a reasonable respect for local customs, it is possible to travel with safety among the pagan tribes of Luzon or in virtually any other part of the Philippines.

Moro lawlessness has been widely publicized. Both organized and sporadic resistance to Spanish law and to American rule has been recorded, but does not apply to all Moslem groups. Banditry and occasional murders of non-Moslems have continued under Filipino rule in parts of the Sulu Islands. In the early 1950's it was considered unsafe for a foreigner to travel more than a few miles from the provincial capital of Jolo. Modern law and order is recognized and has come to command respect, but this respect has developed at a slower pace than elsewhere in the country.

The major law-enforcement problem that remains in Moroland is that of customs control. There are vast waters and miles of isolated coasts to be patrolled. A vinta equipped with an outboard motor can move speedily among the numerous small islands and can cross shallow reefs to escape the larger patrol boats. Illicit entry of aliens or the smuggling of high-value cargo can be profitable to the few individuals who successfully defy government regulations. And the best place to practice this illicit traffic happens to be in the extreme southern Philippines, but for geographic reasons as much as because of the cultural heritage of the area.

THE HUKBALAHAPS

The only organized resistance to the Philippine government has been the Hukbalahaps, commonly called "the Huks." (Hukbalahap is a condensation of a Tagalog phrase, *Huk bo ny Bayan Laban Sa Hapon,* which means "People's Anti-Japanese Army.") This was a Communist-directed group that spread terror and destruction in central Luzon and to a limited extent on a few other islands at mid-century. Composed largely of peasants, but with some intellectuals among the leaders, it was first organized in 1942 to fight and harass the invader. The Huks were a highly effective guerrilla group, and fought continuously and successfully against the Japanese during the three years of occupation. But throughout the war they raided homes of large landowners and those associated with them, ostensibly to obtain supplies for themselves and to "keep rice from falling into the hands of the Japanese." Led by Luis Taruc, a labor organizer and former editor of labor publications, the ideology of the leadership became more openly Communist only in the postwar years. Interested primarily in socio-economic reform, they vigorously opposed the central government and charged that it was in the hands of collaborators and those with vested interests in governmental affairs.

The Huks operated primarily on the Central Plain north of Manila where land reforms were long overdue. (In Pampanga Province 70 percent of the farmers were tenants.) Rents were intolerable, and the peasant level of living was pathetic. The rank and file of the organization were simply discontented peasants and other dissatisfied Filipinos who sought a better life for themselves and their families. They were not Communists nor did they concern themselves with any other specific political philosophy. Simply stated, the disruption accompanying the Japanese occupation of the Philippines, among other things, had permitted the Hukbalahap to assume control and set up a local administration without regard to the national government. First in defiance of the landlords, then of the government which they argued was prejudiced in favor of the landlords, they resisted attempts to pacify or appease them and presented an armed revolt of major significance. The wartime civil administration was thus continued. Whether it was initially Communist-inspired is debatable; nonetheless the movement became Communist-led. There is no proof of Russian direction or the use of Soviet supplies, but the Hukbalahap presented another threat, another avenue of Communist influence and growth in East and Southeast Asia.

This was the stage when President Quirino appointed Ramon Magsaysay as Minister of Defense in September of 1950. The situation was desperate. Huk strength was estimated at 40,000 armed members, many times that number of reserves, and probably several million sympathizers. Magsaysay reorganized and brought a new sense of responsibility to the army. He pursued the Huks deep into the hills and mountains, personally leading the raids on occasion. He fought inefficiency and corruption at all levels. He adopted and followed a policy of all-out friendship for those who would surrender. Huks who had been neither indicted nor convicted by the courts and who desired a farm of their own were offered resettlement on 6 to 10 hectares in newly established communities in Mindanao. Within a year the Huk menace had been markedly reduced. The climax came with the surrender of Luis Taruc to then-President Magsaysay in 1954. Law and order had been restored to central Luzon.

POLITICS AND LEADERSHIP

Before the war a single party, the *Nationalista* party of Manuel Quezon and Sergio Osmeña, dominated all elections. At times the two leaders engaged in political warfare, but the rival factions always adjusted their differences to present a united front on major issues. As a result minor political groups found survival difficult. The history of political parties was one of fusion, merger, and absorption of minorities.

After World War II a two-party system developed. But the two parties (Nationalists and Liberals) are indistinguishable in many respects. In fact, the liberal wing of the Nationalist Party became the new Liberal Party. Both parties are highly personalized, as leaders and followers tend to switch from one to the other. Forceful and dynamic Ramon Magsaysay switched from a Liberal cabinet post in the Quirino administration to lead the Nationalists to victory in 1953.

Factions and splinter groups may loom large on the horizon temporarily, but merger is likely to occur before election time. In 1946 the old Democratic Alliance supported Osmeña at the national level, but elected some representatives in the "Huk territory" of central Luzon. Carlos Romulo's embryonic third party in 1953 joined Magsaysay and the Nationalists well before the November elections. In 1961, Rogelio de la Rosa, an independent candidate for the presidency, withdrew 10 days before the election to back the Liberal candidate, Diosdado Macapagal.

Four parties placed names of national stature on the presidential ballot in 1957, the only time several parties placed candidates in a major election. The campaign was vicious, waged more on the basis of personalities than on issues. It resulted in the election of a Nationalist president, Carlos Garcia, and a Liberal vice president, Macapagal—a rare circumstance, but perfectly legal in the Philippines. Candidates of the third and fourth parties polled a respectable number of votes, but both were splinters from the major parties and both lacked the personal leadership for a continued challenge. (Manuel Manahan, former Nationalist and a devoted disciple of Magsaysay, received 21 percent of the vote, but his newly formed Progressive Party won no national offices.) By 1961, their followers had returned to the fold of the major parties. Fusion and absorption, as in prewar days, continued to be the *modus operandi* for minor political groups. If Philippine political parties appear to be unstable and highly personalized, one is reminded that they are neither as unstable nor as personalized as the parties in most of the other lands of Southeast Asia.

Philippine political parties are free. In any over-all or longtime evaluation they are larger and more important than the men who control them. Only the Communist party has been banned by the Philippine government, and this only after the Huks had resorted to terror and violence. Leaders may be provocative. They may be subject to question or criticism on the basis of professional ethics or personal deeds. The winner on election day may be the man whose followers have spent the most pesos, or the candidate whose workers have been most effective at intimidation of the voters. But the real leaders are those occasional winners who are personally popular with the masses. Manuel Quezon was such a national figure. Ramon Magsaysay won fame because he invited "bare feet to the palace," but he won the presidency because the people across the country believed in him. A one-time mechanic and wartime guerrilla leader, he defeated the Huks and restored peace and order to the country. He appealed to the electorate as a *tao* (common man) who could never forget his humble beginnings. When he campaigned in the barrios, the people loved it. His administration was noted for a peace and reparations treaty with Japan, land reform, the beginning of a public health program, and the surrender of Luis Taruc, leader of the Huks.

President Diosdado Macapagal has some of these same qualities of national popularity and political appeal. As a boy he tended carabao and searched for frogs in the rice paddies, yet did well enough in the neighborhood school to be named valedictorian of his class. His mother raised pigs and took in boarders to help him through the provincial high school.

Macapagal's qualifications for the presidency were outstanding. A lawyer and former law professor, he worked in the office of Commonwealth President Manuel Quezon and later in the Department of Foreign Affairs. He served as a member of the House of Representatives, and was Vice President of the Republic (1958-1962). He has represented his country in the Philippine Embassy in Washington, D.C., as delegate to the Southeast Asia Conference, as member and later chairman of the Philippine delegation to the UN General Assembly, as negotiator and signer of the United States-Philippine Mutual Defense Treaty, as a member of the Philippine delegation to the San Francisco Peace Conference, and as a member of the Laurel economic mission to the United States. His political program is more general and rhetorical than specific. In his election campaign he promised to welcome foreign investment, protect local industry, get government out of nationalized business, and bring "decency and prosperity" to the Philippines. History may subsequently record that he was a truly great president.

The shortage, and shortcomings, of leaders in the Philippines has been a distinct handicap to national growth and to the development of a favorable national image. Charges of nepotism do not build confidence in national leaders. There have been some good and strong leaders. But leadership has not been consistently strong nor always good. Political leaders of strong character and proven stature have been too few in number. This handicap, along with the unreadiness of the people to be led, have retarded the growth of the nation, economically and politically. National fervor is no substitute for literacy, or for an understanding of highly efficient, modern techniques of rice cultivation, or for the ability to foresee that private foreign investors will make direct investments abroad only if there is reasonable potential for gain. To provide mature political leadership or to prepare for rapid economic development requires both education and experience—that is, a breadth of comprehension and understanding.

Economic development is hindered, passively or actively, by the intense conservatism of a large proportion of the population, and particularly the average peasant. Habits and customs die slowly. Drastic reforms, particularly in the fields of taxation and landownership, have come too slowly and painfully. Here nationalism can play a beneficial role. People who are proud of their independence and their country's progress are normally more trustful of their leaders. The populace may acquiesce to revolutionary changes which they would resist strongly if thrust upon them by a colonial power.

But leadership has often been hesitant. Vested interests and personal feelings have, on occasion, taken precedent over national welfare and long-range benefits.

Despite certain obvious negative aspects of Philippine leadership, however, it is far superior to that of most of the postwar new nations. There is a considerable number of Philippine leaders in politics, in agriculture, in education, and in other areas who are well trained by the standards of the country they represent. Filipinos trained abroad number in the thousands, and most of them have a good solid training in an American university. This is so different from and so much greater than the number of properly trained and experienced leaders in the Republic of the Congo, Mali, and most other new African nations; or in Cambodia, Vietnam, and most other Southeast Asian nations. By comparison with Western nations, Philippine leadership at the national level has notable weakness; by comparison with nations of similar geographic resources and political history, the Philippine leadership looks very good indeed.

Other new nations may note that changes in the Philippine Republic have come about by generally peaceful and basically democratic methods. There has been no seizure of power by an angry mob of shouting citizens. Although political maturity in all of its facets has not yet been attained, the adolescent corruption and apathetic leadership of earlier years appear to be largely in the past. Therefore, it should be possible for the people of other new nations to draw reasonable encouragement from the maturing democracy of the Philippines.

Foreign Policy and Foreign Trade

PHILIPPINE foreign policy reflects the American heritage and is based upon close ties with the United States. It also reflects a great respect for and strong loyalty to the United Nations and its specialized agencies. There is an awareness of and a sincere sympathy for the ambitions of dependent peoples on any continent, no doubt a reflection of Filipino nationalist feelings and the recency of Philippine independence. In the "cold war" the Philippines have been consistently pro-Western. There is a genuine fear of international Communism, as it constitutes a potential threat to the continued independence and over-all security of the Republic. Finally, although the Philippines is considered to be the most Westernized country in Asia and it looks to the West in many ways, there is a basic realization that the country is geographically a part of Asia and that relations with its neighbors must reflect the facts of location and position. In a sense, regionalism conflicts with internationalism, and neither is completely compatible with nationalism. Philippine foreign policy, then, is both idealistic and realistic, and the Philippine image tends to reflect certain conflicts of interest and feeling. However, in any "showdown situation" idealism has given way to realism.

PHILIPPINE ROLE IN THE UNITED NATIONS

The Philippines has been an active participant in the United Nations from its very beginning, the only charter member from Southeast Asia. The Philippine delegation to the United Nations has consistently had superior leadership. Carlos Romulo was chairman of the Philippine delegation to the San Francisco Conference on International Organization in 1945; he was permanent Philippine delegate to the United Nations from 1946 until 1953 and much of the time since then. He was elected president of its General Assembly in 1949, which can be considered a tribute both to his country and to him. Diosdado Macapagal, now President Macapagal, was a delegate (in 1950) and chairman (1951) of the Philippine delegation to the UN General Assembly. The Philippines was elected to membership on the Trusteeship Council for 1948-1950 and again in 1955, in the latter case sharing a "split-term" with Yugoslavia. The Filipinos are proud of the United Nations flag that flies over a small building on Isaac Peral (Street) in Manila.

The Philippines took an active part in the Korean peace action. Even before the Communist invasion the Republic supported the early recommendations of the United Nations on Korea, participated in Korean commissions under the auspices of the world organization, and recognized the Republic of Korea. The invasion of South Korea on June 25, 1950, provoked a war scare in Manila. The actions of the Security Council of the United Nations met with favor and immediate support in the Philippine press. Some Filipino veterans and former Philippine Scouts tried to volunteer for duty in Korea with the U. S. armed forces. Medicines and food supplies were offered. Because of the seriousness of the Hukbalahap problem and because of the then financial crisis, the Quirino administration was reluctant to send forces out of the country. But in early August both the Senate and the House of Representatives voted unanimously to send armed forces to the battle front. As a result of this action, approximately 5,000 volunteer officers and men organized into regimental combat teams were sent to Korea after undergoing rigorous training in the foothills of the Sierra Madre a few miles from Manila. Subsequently, the Philippines was a member of the United Nations Commission for the Unification and Rehabilitation of Korea; it approved the armistice of July 27, 1953 that ended the Korean fighting; and it joined with the 15 other UN nations having armed forces in Korea in a declaration that they would resist a renewal of the attack.

The Republic has maintained an active role in many of the specialized international agencies and is a member of most of them. Filipinos are pleased to be treated as equals, to participate in an organization where their vote, or that of any small nation, is the equal of the vote of the United States or the Soviet Union. The work of the World Health Organization and UNICEF in the Philippines has been recognized with gratitude and sincere appreciation. The Philippine National Commission on UNESCO has been a very active organization, and the UNESCO Regional Scientific Office was welcomed to Manila when it could no longer operate in Shanghai. Philippine politicians are pleased to be appointed as delegates to UN meetings or commissions. Filipinos are proud of the help received from the United Nations Technical Assistance Administration in providing specialists in various aspects of education, to help up-grade Philippine education. They would be glad for more, rather than less of the United Nations.

NATION-TO-NATION RELATIONS

In addition to active participation in the United Nations and adherence to its principles, Philippine foreign policy is based upon a three-fold set of objectives—namely, (1) to maintain, deepen, and broaden Philippine-United States relations, (2) to maintain and improve good neighbor relations with other Asian countries, and (3) to maintain and continually improve the historical relationship with Spain and other Latin countries. To this group should be added still another, although unstated principle—namely, to encourage the freedom of colonial peoples everywhere. Toward this end the Philippines looked with favor upon the formation of the new state of Indonesia, opened legations in the then-new countries of Pakistan and India very shortly after Philippine independence, was among the first countries to recognize South Vietnam, Cambodia, and Laos, and has been sympathetic to the independence of colonial peoples in Africa.

The third stated objective is somewhat more sentimental than practical. It appeals to the Spanish element of the population, reflecting a certain pride of Filipinos in the culture acquired during Spanish rule and which survived American administration. But few Filipinos are personally interested in Spain or in other Latin countries, and foreign trade with Spain is meager. However, in the United Nations the Philippines was one of several countries that sponsored a resolution, adopted November 4, 1950, to lift the 1946 ban on Spanish participation in conferences and the UN specialized agencies. In 1955 the Philippines supported the admission of Spain to the United Nations. And the two countries maintain embassies, rather than legations, in each other's capital city. Basically, relations between the Philippines and Spain are more cultural than either economic or political.

THE TWO CHINAS

The Philippines has been consistently hostile toward Communism and does not maintain diplomatic relations with the Soviet Union or any other Communist state. Philippine failure to recognize the People's Republic of China, then, is not only consistent with national attitude and established policy toward Communism, but also in line with U. S. policy toward Peking. The late Senator Recto, whose views were pro-Asian, favored trade with Communist China upon her attainment of UN membership, and the Chinese Communist press has urged normal relations between the two countries. However, neither voice has carried any influence with Malacañang or the Office of Foreign Affairs. The present policy can be maintained without difficulty so long as Taiwan remains under control of the Nationalists and the United States continues to recognize the Taipei government. If the Communists should win Taiwan, the Philippines would be placed in the precarious position of having an unrecognized Communist state within 200 miles of the northern islets of the country. If Washington should recognize Red China, the Filipinos would find themselves in conflict between close association with the United States on matters of world politics and their own avowed anti-Communist front. It is conceivable, then, that Philippine policy toward Communist China could change, but it is unlikely to do so unless there is a change in basic factors over which the Filipinos have no control.

The Republic of the Philippines has continued to recognize the Nationalist government of China, but relations with Taiwan have not always been smooth. A treaty of amity was signed between the two countries in April, 1947, and Generalissimo Chiang Kai-shek visited President Elpidio Quirino in 1949. In the United Nations the Philippines has consistently supported the Nationalist government in its efforts to represent China and to exclude the Peking regime from the UN. It voted to brand Communist China an aggressor in Korea and called for an embargo on strategic war materials to her and to North Korea. But there are at least 350,000, possibly half a million, Chinese in the Philippines. Their investments in the Philippine Republic probably amount to more than $100 million. Their economic position has caused the Philippine government to restrict Chinese activities, especially in retail trade, despite a strong protest from Nationalist China.

Closely associated with Philippine policy toward Taiwan is a quiet fear about the political sympathy of the Chinese minority. There is no reason to believe that the vast majority is not loyal to Nationalist China. Membership in the Chinese Communist organization in the Philippines is small, its funds are limited, and its political activities are illegal. However, there is a constant fear that Chinese Communists are being smuggled into the country through the southern islands by way of Kalimantan (Borneo).

The Chinese schools have been still another source of irritation. They are suspected of being centers of Communist infiltration, and they are charged with following curricula prescribed by the Nationalist government in Taipei, rather than those prescribed by the Philippine Department of Education. Reportedly, children of Chinese immigrants have become Philippine citizens without acquiring a knowledge of the country's history, government, or customs. This is, of course, contrary to the national policy of Filipinization. All fears and charges may be over-exaggerated at the present time. Taipei is as much concerned about Communist infiltration as is Manila and will do all it can do to prevent it. Any significant indoctrination is most unlikely. After considerable diplomatic discussion, China has conceded the exclusive jurisdiction of the Philippine government over all schools, but with a kind of "joint supervision" over the 137 Chinese schools. More specifically, on January 23, 1956, it was agreed that the Philippine authorities will prescribe the basic curricula, but the schools may offer additional subjects. Generally speaking, this places the Chinese schools in the same position as the American School in Manila and the numerous church-controlled primary and secondary schools.

SOUTHEAST ASIAN COUNTRIES

Filipinos are trying to develop close ties with their immediate neighbors in Southeast Asia. The Philippines has been the host to a number of regional meetings. The University of the Philippines agricultural and forestry campus at Los Baños, which is well known in Southeast Asia, has repeatedly had students from nearby nations and territories. By means of a program of Southeast Asian scholarships, an Institute of Asian Studies at the Quezon City campus encourages graduate students from Asian nations. At the government level, high officials of the Philippines and neighboring countries have exchanged visits. In 1952, for example, President Sukarno of Indonesia visited the Philippines and addressed the Philippine Congress. A few months later President Quirino returned the visit. Carlos Garcia, then Vice-President and Secretary of Foreign Affairs, visited Thailand, Vietnam, and Pakistan on state business, and he was in Australia for the Canberra Conference of SEATO ministers when he was called home to take the oath of the presidency.

Nonetheless, those countries of Southeast Asia that follow a neutralist foreign policy view the Philippines with some misgivings because of Manila's strong stand against Communism. Those countries that have recently overthrown European colonialism by other than peaceful means have a strong anti-European (anti-Caucasian) feeling and view with some distrust the close Philippine ties with America. There may be more than a little envy of the Filipino and his somewhat greater fluency in English at an international gathering. There is a feeling that the Filipinos regard themselves as superior to their neighbors because they are more Westernized. Even though the Philippines has close and meaningful ties with its neighbors in many ways, there are some elements of difference; no realistic Southeast Asian counterpart of either NATO or the Common Market is about to be formed.

Friendship ties and smooth relations between the Philippines and *Indonesia* are particularly important, and they are based upon a variety of common factors. The two peoples have a common racial and linguistic background and a similar historical heritage. Spanish and American rule in the Philippines was not radically different than that of the Portuguese and the Dutch in the Indies. Both had known a national pride that had sparked and smoldered during an extended colonial regime. Both felt the heel of Japan. Both entered the world community of nations very shortly after the Japanese had been defeated. The fact that their dominant religion is markedly different can be only a very minor irritant. It has never marred either political or economic relations between the two countries; neither country has coveted or otherwise been particularly concerned about the minority religious group (Philippine Moslems or Indonesian Christians) within the domain of the other country.

The major problem for negotiation has been smuggling and the illegal entrance of aliens. Both peoples are Malays; they have a similar appearance, speak a similar dialect, and possess many similar customs; therefore, they can be readily assimilated into the populace of the other country and normally constitute no real threat to law and order. Although there is a substantial number of people who are of Philippine ancestry in Sabah (the Sandakan area), Filipinos have not traveled to Indonesia in great numbers and have not posed a real problem for Indonesian officials. However, for purpose of trade or to improve their economic opportunity, Indonesians for decades, possibly centuries, have moved northward into the southern Philippines. The six thousand or so illegal Indonesian immigrants in the Philippines have caused some fears that Communists may have been included, or that this avenue of approach might be used by Communists at some future time. By the establishment of a Philippine consulate in Sulawesi (Celebes) and an Indonesian vice-consulate at Davao, it is hoped to reduce somewhat both the illegal entry of aliens and the smuggling activities for which the waters of the southern Philippines have become well known.

The Philippines supported Indonesian independence in the domestic press and on the floor of the United Nations. Moreover, Carlos Romulo took an active part in the New Delhi Conference on Indonesia in January, 1949. Yet there are obvious differences in national policy and outlook. The military association of the Philippines with the United States and the West is not appreciated in

Indonesia, which has no substantial ties with either the West or the Communist bloc. And the Philippines does not appreciate Indonesian foreign policy with respect to the Communist world.

The Philippines generally avoided public statements on the West Irian (Netherlands New Guinea) controversy. In no sense was this remnant of Dutch colonialism in the Southwest Pacific a strain on the Philippines. Because of its anti-colonial outlook, the Manila government was sympathic to Indonesian efforts to acquire West Irian. Yet, Philippine authorities could not ignore the fact that the native Papuans were not Indonesians; for whom the change represents a substitution of Indonesian rule for Dutch rule. And this change of rulership was strongly opposed by Australia, a member of the Manila Pact and friend of the Philippines.

As neighboring insular republics, both Indonesia and the Philippines recognize the desirability of unity between them. If either should fall to a hostile state, the security of the other would be seriously endangered. They may differ on some world issues, or they may use a different approach to a common problem, but basically the two must work together or each will become more vulnerable to outside aggressive forces.

Toward *Vietnam, Cambodia,* and *Laos* Philippine policy has been sympathetic, but cautious. Cambodia and Laos were recognized by Manila on July 8, 1955, Vietnam six days later. A Filipino was an advisor on the constitution of Vietnam. A Philippine minister to the three states maintains residence in Saigon. But if a Filipino wishes to visit the ancient edifices of Angkor, he must go to Bangkok or Saigon for his Cambodian *visa;* it cannot be obtained in Manila. At one time the Philippines encouraged the three states to join SEATO, but without success. Trade negotiations have been held and agreements reached, but the results are more technical than fruitful, for these countries do not complement each other economically. Speeches of Prince Norodom Sihanorek of Cambodia during his official visit to the Philippines in 1956 and published accounts of his remarks after he returned home left Filipino leaders with mixed emotions. At best, they were convinced that he was a neutralist with Communist sympathies, which did not make pleasant news in the anti-Communist Philippines.

Actually, people-to-people relationships have been more meaningful than government-to-government actions. Under "Operation Brotherhood" a group of young Filipinos, primarily doctors and nurses, went to Vietnam in 1954 to assist refugees from north of the seventeenth parallel. Supported largely by the Philippine Junior Chamber of Commerce and the Philippine Red Cross, which supplies transportation costs and medical supplies, this group of volunteers has continued as a kind of private Filipino Peace Corps. On occasion, the U. S. Operations Mission to Cambodia has employed Filipinos for work in Cambodia. Many Vietnamese students study in the Philippines—49 of the 408 Vietnamese students abroad in 1956 were in the island republic.

The views of *Thailand* and the Philippines are similar in many ways. Both countries have a Chinese minority, and both have passed legislation aimed at restricting or retarding Chinese control of certain aspects of the economy. Both fear Communism and have aligned themselves with the United States in efforts to contain it within its present confines. Both countries are charter members of the SEATO alliance, primarily designed to thwart Communism, and both would like to see other Southeast Asian countries in this or some similar regional organization. Like the Philippines, Thailand was not on the initial invitation list to join the Colombo Plan, probably because it was considered to be too closely associated with Western powers. The request for and acceptance of large amounts of economic aid from the United States and the presence of U. S. forces along with large quantities of equipment and supplies in Thailand in connection with the Laotian crisis in 1962 is indicative of these ties and somewhat parallels the Philippine situation.

Burma's foreign policy contrasts markedly with that of Thailand and is somewhat comparable to that of Indonesia. But from the Philippine standpoint, Burma is not a near neighbor. It is 1,700 miles from Manila to Rangoon, and there is no direct route between the two capitals. The Philippines has not approved of the neutralist attitude of U Nu and other Burmese leaders, of the several rice pacts with Communist countries, of the scholarships for Burmese elementary teachers at Moscow University, or of many other actions of the Burmese government. But, because Burma is physically farther removed, the Filipinos are less concerned about Burmese affairs than with the affairs of any other Southeast Asian state. Contact between Rangoon and Manila can best be described as occasional, rather than frequent.

In foreign relations *Malaya* (and Malaysia) has been closely associated with Great Britain. The decision to remain in the Commonwealth of Nations and to permit Commonwealth forces to remain in Malaya is indicative of this close association. The influence of the United States is strong, but not conspicuous, and is more economic than political. Hence, political relations with the Philippines or any other Southeast Asian country have been minimal. Nonetheless, Malaya and the Philippines have much in common. Both experienced a Communist-led uprising that was defeated only after protracted fighting, and both fear Communists among the Chinese minority. Both are strong advocates of the United Nations and its specialized agencies. In foreign policy Malaysia, like the Philippines and Thailand, is strongly with the West.

Malaya and the Philippines both supported an economic Association of Southeast Asian States (ASAS). First proposed by President Garcia and Prime Minister Rehman, the ASAS would not be political or military and would not compete with SEATO; instead, it would be a means of economic and cultural collaboration among the countries of the area. Malaya's Premier and the principal foreign affairs officers of the Philippines and Thailand agreed in February, 1961, to establish a joint working group to study the matter. Except for Indonesia, the nations have responded favorably to the proposal.

Philippine relations with the countries of Southwest Asia, the Indian sub-continent, and Australia have been nominal. Because of its stronger Western attitude and membership in SEATO, Pakistan is regarded somewhat more warmly than India. There is little in common between the Philippines and the Arab states of Southwest Asia and Africa, except a common sympathy for dependent peoples. Hence, the Philippines has looked with favor upon the creation of the new nations of the past decade, and because of the Philippine Moslems' interest in Mecca there is an increasing official interest in the Moslem states of the Near and Middle East. The establishment of Philippine diplomatic relations with Israel is further evidence of a growing concern in the Eastern Mediterranean. The Philippines and Australia are allies under the Manila Pact, but apart from security, common ties are limited. The so-called "White Australia" policy is somewhat of a barrier, and the great distance between Manila and Canberra offers an additional handicap. Even economic relations are limited: some abaca and a little copra are shipped to Australia, and small amounts of frozen meat and wheat or flour to the Philippines.

RELATIONS WITH JAPAN

The anti-Japanese feeling that was so prevalent, and justifiably so, immediately after the war has diminished considerably in the past few years. Nonetheless, Philippine relations with Japan have been noticeably less cordial than her dealings with the nations of Southeast Asia. As a member of the Far East Commission, the Philippines had a share in making policy toward occupied Japan. The new republic stressed a "tough" policy in any Japanese settlement.

This attitude results in part from a natural fear that the once-militant Japanese may again seek to create a "New Order" in eastern Asia. It reflects the fact that before the Pacific War about 30,000 Japanese lived in the Philippines, where they dominated abaca production in the Davao area. Their total investments in the Philippines were estimated at $25 to 30 million in 1941; hence, there is a real fear of Japanese economic competition. Probably there is a reflection of or a relationship to the general attitude in the Orient that "to the victor belongs the spoils." In that part of the world it has been the practice to defeat a man, a people, or a country; then keep him down, if possible. Tribute or other evidence of subjugation has been standard operating procedure throughout history. But most of all, the immediate postwar "tough" attitude reflected recent memories of Japanese harshness during the three and one-half years of occupation—the death of loved ones, the personal embarrassments, the shortage of basic necessities of life, and the tremendous physical destruction to Manila and other cities at the time of liberation. But time has a way of healing the wounds of wartime harshness and atrocities. Moreover, the new generation cannot remember them. There is also a realistic awareness that both Japan and the Philippines are on the rim of Asia, that they have much in common, that their goals and aspirations are more complementary than competitive. So, there has been a renewal of relations with Japan, both diplomatic and economic.

Commercial relations between the two countries redeveloped gradually and for a time functioned erratically. The first trade was subject to barter arrangements periodically extended. The first Japanese ship to return to Philippine waters came for a cargo of logs in September, 1950. It docked at a lumber company in Basilan, a small island in the far south that had not experienced the ravages of war or the harshness of occupation so generally true elsewhere in the Archipelago. The next year Japanese freighters with the famous "Maru" markings were seen in other southern ports and also loaded logs at Aparri in the far north. Japanese products appeared in some shops in small amounts in the middle 1950's, but it was not until 1957 that Japanese trade representatives re-established offices in Manila and Japanese nationals moved about with freedom. (Japanese workers involved in the salvage of sunken vessels in Manila Bay, a result of an interim agreement on reparations that was signed in April, 1953, were required to live on-ship without shore leave at any time. The first postwar Japanese student in the Philippines enrolled at the state university in 1957.)

The reparations issue presented the greatest problem to Philippine-Japanese relations. Under the terms of the peace treaty Japan accepted the obligation to pay reparations in goods and services, but no amount was specified. This was left to determination by bilateral negotiation between the occupied countries and Japan. The "tough" policy of the Philippines made these negotiations a difficult and lengthy process; negotiations that began with exploratory talks by the representatives of the two countries to the Japanese Peace Conference in San Francisco, September 4-8, 1951, finally ended with the signing of a reparations agreement on May 9, 1956.

In summary, this agreement specified that Japan provide within a maximum period of 20 years $550 million worth of reparations—$500 million in capital goods, $30 million in services, and $20 million in the form of price reductions on items that the Philippines buys from

Japan in normal trade. In a separate but closely related agreement the Japanese government consented to obtain from private industrialists not more than $250 million in long-term credits for capital goods, these credits to be made available to Philippine private enterprise. Ultimately these agreements will result in closer economic relations between Japan and the Philippines and their respective business firms. In fact, they have already contributed to increased Philippine-Japanese trade and to increased Philippine industrialization.

The Philippine Senate had refused to approve the San Francisco peace treaty until the reparations issue was settled. With the final approval of the reparations agreement, the way was open for the approval of the treaty and the establishment of normal relations between the two countries. On July 16, 1956, the Senate of the Philippines gave its formal consent to the Japanese peace treaty of 1951. The war between Japan and the Philippines was officially over, and Felino Neri, former Under Secretary and Acting Secretary of Foreign Affairs, was appointed the first ambassador to Japan. Relations between the two countries are still formal, but their tone is now much more cordial.

STATUS OF NATIONAL BOUNDARIES

As an insular republic with well-defined geometric boundaries, the Philippines has exercised a greater freedom of action than is generally true of continental states. The Philippines has claimed jurisdiction over all waters within the treaty limits which, except in the vicinity of Kalimantan (Borneo), are well beyond any inhabited islands. This has led to considerable criticism, for Philippine claims extend well beyond a 3-mile limit, or even a 12-mile limit, from insular shores. Thus they are in direct violation of the Geneva Convention of 1958.

The only boundary problems have been in the southwest—the Turtle Islands and North Borneo. Under provisions of the Anglo-American convention and notes that were signed January 2, 1930, American sovereignty over the Turtle Islands and the nearby Mangsee Islands was recognized by Great Britain, but administration of them was left to the British North Borneo Company unless and

until the American government gave notice of its desire to ad-
minister them. Since the center of the Turtle Islands is less than
30 miles from Sandakan, the prewar capital of the British area, and
the Mangsee Islands are only a little farther north and west, British
interests were real. They were concerned about proper police action
and the operation of a lighthouse along the western approach to
Sandakan harbor. On September 19, 1946, after the Philippines
received its independence, the Manila government officially informed Great Britain of its desire to assume the administration of
the islands. The British again expressed some fears about police
action and the lighthouse (not then in operation). The Philippines
took over administration of the Turtle and Mangsee Islands on
October 16, 1947, giving assurance that a proper police force would
be maintained and expressing willingness to lease the lighthouse
site to North Borneo for one peso per year for as long as the British
needed the facility.

Of greater potential consequence, however, is the controversy
over ownership of North Borneo. It merits close observation and
could imperil the British-supported federation of Malaysia. In 1946
the "North Borneo Question" was considered by the Philippine
Foreign Office, the Office of Legal Affairs, and other interested
parties. The subject was not pushed at that time because it was felt
that the Sultan, his heirs, or his successor should ask the Philippine
government on behalf of the sultanate to protest to Britain the
absorption of North Borneo. But the sultan had died, his heirs were
not readily identifiable, and the Moros could not agree on who
should succeed to the throne.

The controversy hinges on one basic question: Did Sultan Maho-
met Jamal Al Alam, the Sultan of Sulu in 1878, lease or cede the
territory of North Borneo, now Sabah, to two British businessmen,
then the owners of the British North Borneo Company. That the
Britons had later turned their rights and interests over to the British
government, and that in 1946 the British government had changed
the status of the area in question to a crown colony, are accessory
facts, but not the basic issue.

The British considered their position legally sound, so they were
startled when, in 1962, the Philippines publicly claimed North

Borneo. The claim is based upon the fact that Sulu was formerly a separate state and that it included much of what was then the colony of North Borneo, that the latter territory was leased rather than ceded by negotiations between the Sultan of Sulu and the British North Borneo Company, and that since Sulu is now a part of the Philippines, the latter has succeeded to Sulu's sovereign rights.

On January 28, 1963, the Philippines formally presented their claim in London. And in Manila, President Macapagal, heretofore publicly silent on the new Malaysia, denounced the Malaysian federation and said that North Borneo is vital to Philippine security. Three days later Britain rejected the Philippine claim, but agreed to discuss the problem and also a program of mutual security for the disputed area. It appears that British ownership of North Borneo may have been open to question. And now that West Irian appears to be firmly in the hands of Indonesia, a fourth country has become interested in the former British Territories in Borneo. Indonesia hailed the "Brunei freedom fighters" of December, 1961. No doubt Sukarno would like to add all of Borneo to Indonesia, but he does not dare to invade. He hoped to induce the United Nations to step in and placate him as it did with Western New Guinea so that Indonesia would not need to fight for what Sukarno wants. But the UN turned a deaf ear. Malaysia appears to be on a solid legal foundation, and Philippine claims on former North Borneo have receded into the background.

FOREIGN TRADE

A large part of the national income of the Philippines traditionally has derived from exports and from United States government payments. Generally the Philippines had a very favorable trade balance in prewar years. In the immediate postwar years, however, there was a relatively smaller volume of exports and a much greater quantity of imports. The resultant net trade deficit necessitated the rigid import controls that were instituted in 1950. Governmental control has been exercised by a direct prohibition of certain commodities and by a kind of quota system under which specific quantities of other goods are permitted to enter into the trade of

the Republic. These controls, with minor alterations and modifica-
tions, remained in effect until 1962, and some of them are still in
force.

The leading exports are coconut products and sugar, followed
by abaca, base metals and concentrates, logs and lumber, canned
pineapple, and tobacco products. Commodity imports still exceed
exports, but by a smaller margin than was true a decade ago. Cotton
and cotton manufactures are normally the leading import, followed by petroleum and petroleum products, iron and steel manufactures, grains and grain products, dairy products, paper, and
chemicals. Imports of rice, tobacco, fish, and fertilizer have declined
significantly in recent years as the production of these commodities
has increased within the Republic. And there has been a marked
decrease in imports of cotton manufactured goods and petroleum
products to coincide with an increase in imports of raw cotton,
cotton yarn, and crude petroleum, a reflection of the newer manufacturing industries in the Philippines.

As the largest foreign consumer of Philippine products, the
United States normally purchases all of the sugar exports; most of
the coconut oil, desiccated coconut, canned pineapple, and embroidery; at least half of the base metals and copra; about 40 percent
of the abaca; and one-fourth of the lumber. The Philippines is now
the main source of imported cigars for American smokers. (In 1961
Cuba supplied 56 percent of the cigars imported into the United
States, but by 1962 the Philippines supplied 58 percent, double the
1961 imports from the Pacific Republic.) Japan is the second-ranking
market for Philippine products, and its relative position has been
improving since 1955. Japan is the sole market for Philippine iron
ore, imports some Philippine copper concentrates and chromite, and
is still the principal market for Philippine logs and lumber although
log exports have declined markedly in recent years. Abaca has a
world-wide market; Philippine copra is shipped to western Europe,
Latin America and Hong Kong; small amounts of leaf tobacco are
marketed in Spain and, on occasion, in Hong Kong; and canned
pineapple has been shipped to West Germany.

The United States has supplied most of the Philippine imports
of machinery, dairy products, cotton and textiles, paper, drugs,

automobiles, and tobacco (largely for blending in the Philippine cigarette industry); also much of the grains and cereal products, petroleum products, and certain kinds of steel products. Japan has become increasingly more important for textiles, transport equipment, and electrical appliances. Indonesia is the principal source of the crude petroleum for Philippine refineries. Western European countries are gradually becoming more important for dairy products, machinery, some steel products, and automobiles. Canada and Australia export wheat and flour to the Philippines. Meats from Australia or Argentina and butter from New Zealand are commonplace in Manila frozen-food stores.

In summary, the United States is still the Philippines most important trading partner, but American-Philippine trade has declined markedly. When, in 1956, U. S. trade dropped to only 57 percent of the Philippine total, it was the lowest percentage recorded since 1916. It is obvious that the Republic has been seeking and finding wider markets for its products and procuring more and more of its needs from countries other than the United States. This is the result of a political decision—to avoid dependence upon a single distant country. It was parallel, but related, to the decision to develop industries, in order to avoid dependence upon continued export of basic raw materials. These political decisions, and the observable results of them, do much to explain the character of the nation and to indicate a kind of leadership among its Southeast Asian neighbors.

11   *The Philippines and the United States*

Americans have a deep interest in the Philippines. It stems from historical factors, from economic attachments, and from military ties, both past and present. It is related to common goals on the international scene.

But this interest is also a result of personal association. A large number of Americans have lived or worked in the Philippines— as members of the armed forces beginning in 1898; as teachers or missionaries; as employees of a mining company, a lumber mill, a sugar *central,* a pineapple or coconut plantation, a shipping firm, a bank, or an airline; or as a representative of the United States government with an assignment to the American Embassy, to the United States Information Agency (formerly USIS) or the Voice of America, or to the United States AID program or one of its predecessors. In 1963 there were more than 600 Peace Corps workers in the Philippines.

The number of Filipinos who have visited the United States is equally impressive. They have come to work on the sugar plantations of Hawaii or in the vegetable fields of California, as employees at the military installations in Guam or elsewhere, as members of the U. S. armed forces (prior to Philippine independence), as students at American colleges and universities, for technical training in government or industry, and for a variety of other reasons. No country other than the Philippines has had as many Filipino residents as has the United States, and no other Asian country has had as many American residents as has the Philippines. The number of Filipinos whom we have known and the number of Filipinos who have known us have created a broad bond of personal friendship.

This deep human interest developed during the half century when the Philippines was an American protegé. It became even stronger during the darkest days of World War II when the Philippines was our staunch ally in the Pacific. It has continued into the postwar years as the people of the two countries have worked side by side for the military, educational, or economic welfare of the new country.

MILITARY TIES AND STRATEGIC RELATIONSHIPS

But American concern for the Philippines is not merely a sentimental attachment flavored with personal relationships. Both interest and international friendship demand that America maintain a deep interest in the welfare of the Philippines. The 1,100-mile archipelago along the southeastern margin of Asia is of extreme strategic importance to America and to all free nations. The Philippines forms the southern link of a natural line of defense extending northward through Taiwan, Okinawa, and Japan. In recognition of their need for each other, the United States and the Philippines signed a treaty of mutual defense in August of 1951. Essentially this was a formal expression of established facts as both the President of the United States and the Secretary of State had declared publicly that they would regard an attack upon the Philippines as an attack upon the United States.

Not only vital to our Pacific defense, the Philippines is *prima facie* evidence of our democratic integrity. In its independence, attained in accordance with promises made by the United States government, the Philippines is proof to the world that the democratic principle is valid and that the United States stands back of its promises. Other peoples, especially other peoples in Asia, have watched developments in the Philippines with interest—in some cases, with envy.

After the Spanish-American War the United States established military bases in the Philippines, and under the Bases Agreement of 1947 continued to maintain them. The principal installations are Clark Air Force Base and the Navy bases at Sangley Point and Subic Bay. Camp John Hay Leave and Recreation Center at Baguio is a mountain rest and rehabilitation center for all American forces in Eastern Asia. The various other bases mentioned in the 1946 Bases Agreement were relinquished to the Philippines in 1959. Those that remain are now held by the United States under long-term lease, and most of the thorny problems of use and jurisdiction have been resolved to mutual satisfaction.

American military assistance to the Philippines, first permitted under the public law approved June 26, 1946, has been far greater than the maintenance of specified bases that are manned by American personnel, however. Since the liberation period (1945-1946) there has been direct aid in many ways. As American forces were removed, their installations and much of the equipment and supplies attached to them were turned over to the Philippine government. Subsequent arrangements were made whereby the Philippines received assistance under the American military aid program, and considerable American equipment and material were supplied to Philippine forces. The Joint United States Military Advisory Group (JUSMAG) became quite active. Its personnel assisted in the development and training of the Filipino armed forces, and some of its members served as instructors at the Armed Forces Institute of the Philippines. In addition a number of Philippine officers and men have attended American service schools. American photographic planes and U. S. Army field parties gathered the information from which Philippine topographic maps were prepared. Military aid to the Philippines between 1945 and June 30, 1962, was valued at more than $400 million.

The significance of American bases and forces in the Philippines and American military aid to the Republic should not be underestimated. The Philippines are tied to and have become a part of the American security system in the Pacific. Clark Field and Subic Bay could become enemy targets in wartime, or sites from which the United States Seventh Fleet and the United States Thirteenth Air Force might operate against a common enemy anywhere between the Formosa Straits and the Bay of Bengal. The Filipino people were in favor of granting these bases. They have looked with favor on the assistance received, for it relieves the Republic from the financial burden and political hazards of maintaining large military and naval forces.

ECONOMIC RELATIONSHIPS

American economic relations with the Philippines have passed through many stages of development and have been governed, successively, by various Acts of Congress and, more recently, by

Philippine legislation. Notwithstanding the complexity and variety of legislative expressions, from whatever origin, the economic relationship has evolved in a reasonably logical fashion. After the acquisition of the Philippines, American capital was invested in the coconut, abaca, sugar, tobacco, mineral, and lumber resources of the new colony, and the products of this investment were marketed in America. By the establishment of free trade between the Philippines and the United States in 1909, the economy of the Islands was effectively tied to that of the parent country. As a result the Philippines became almost entirely dependent upon United States markets for the disposition of export products—namely, raw materials. Under these circumstances, it was equally logical that the Philippine colony import its manufactured goods primarily from America. The Philippines, therefore, became an economic as well as a political dependency of the United States. There was one primary difference. Over a period of almost half a century there was an attempt to prepare the Filipinos for political independence, but there was no realistic attempt to prepare the colony for economic independence. Therein lay the basis for a part of the fiscal pitfalls of the Philippine Republic after independence had been attained. The economy of the Philippines is still intricately related to the United States. Some of the earlier financial interests and trade relationships have been retained or reestablished in a different form after Japanese occupation and postwar independence. New American private capital for other purposes, primarily manufacturing, has entered the Philippine economic arena within the past dozen years or so. It has bolstered the national economy and helped reduce imports from whatever source, because new Philippine manufacturing is primarily for the domestic market.

The Philippines have been the recipient of large amounts of American economic aid, more than three times the amount of military aid received. Still it is markedly less than that given to Japan, Korea, or Nationalist China.

In the Philippines, economic and technical assistance is a long-range proposition. Aside from those benefits outlined at the time of independence, it began with the appointment of three agricultural specialists early in the Point IV program in 1950. Economic aid has since ranged through various kinds of assistance—in agriculture, particularly land reform, agricultural extension work, and irrigation projects; in transportation, for road construction in frontier areas and for port development and harbor improvement; in assistance to industry, primarily in the form of hydroelectric installations and industrial planning; and in education, largely scholarships and travel grants in the area of industrial and technical education.

The Philippine economy is basically sound. In view of the lack of industry prior to independence, economic expansion has taken place at a rapid rate. The swift growth of the economy represents a joint effort of American capital, technical know-how, and economic assistance, on the one hand, and Philippine administrative policy and its associated austerity program, along with somewhat more limited Philippine capital investment, on the other. Whatever the ultimate result, it can be credited to economic bilateralism.

POLITICAL AND SOCIAL ASSOCIATIONS

Early American government in the Philippines was a benevolent paternalism. Americans concerned themselves with health and sanitation, economic development, and a public education system. Schoolteachers came in substantial numbers to work alongside public health officials. Army men resigned and remained in the Philippines to seek fame and fortune in mining, real estate, or agriculture, and some of them married Filipinas. Businessmen came to establish American interests in lumber, sugar, or other lines. There was a succession of capable American administrators with a devoted parental attitude toward public welfare.

Philippine schools are not American schools, but they have marked similarities. Educational ties between the two countries are strong. Initially American teachers were used throughout the system. Filipinos who began their schooling in 1900 may have had only American teachers from first grade through college. Their children in turn may have had mostly Filipino teachers who had been taught by American teachers. Today, the United States and its citizens still occupy a significant role in Philippine education. Among the missionary schools and colleges there are many that are staffed in part by American personnel. The Fulbright Program and the AID program in education bring American professors to the Philippines and help Filipinos to obtain higher education at American universities and colleges. Many Peace Corps members work in Philippine schools. U. S. war damage funds helped to rebuild Philippine libraries; the books on their shelves may have been purchased from either Philippine or American funds, but the majority of them were published in America.

The Philippine government is patterned after the American system and dedicated to democratic processes. The Constitution specifically guarantees the rights and properties of foreign nationals. The special rights and privileges granted American citizens engaged in business in the Philippines under the so-called "parity rights" were incorporated into the Philippine-American trade agreement and written into the Philippine Constitution.

Philippine-American relations are important in Manila and in Washington. They have been cordial and fruitful. In only a few instances has it been impossible to reconcile differences in national interests, and these few differences have not visibly affected the basic relationships and commitments that were established at the time of Philippine independence. One of the delicate problems of recent years has been largely settled. It included the payment of the gold-devaluation claim for $23 million and the successful negotiations for the revision of the military bases agreement which resulted in: (1) the transfer of the Olongapo community to the Philippines; (2) the reduction of the lease period of American bases from 99 years to 25 years; (3) the relinquishment of considerable area previously under American control and the precise delimitation of boundaries for those areas retained; and (4) the assurance of prior consultation with the Philippine government before any U. S. construction of missile launching sites in the Philippines.[1]

The foreign policy of the Philippines is based upon close ties with the United States. The Filipino may criticize his country's close association with a nation that lies an ocean away, but he would not have it otherwise. The American on the street corner may voice a similar opposition, but he is forced to recognize that in the bipolar

[1] Carlos Romulo, "The Philippines Since Independence," *Current History,* Vol. 40, 1961, p. 146.

world of today a strong ally in Southeast Asia is very important indeed. There is no contradiction between the United States emphasis on security and the Philippine emphasis on economic and social development. American military aid and defense support has helped to free greater Philippine resources for other purposes—education, land reform and agricultural research, industrial growth, and community development.

In summation, the Philippines is a part of Asia geographically, and the Filipinos are of Asia racially. Hence, as President Garcia stated in 1960, they must make every effort to develop closer relations with fellow Asians, never forgetting that in unity lies strength. However, the United States and the Philippines are united by historical, economic, and military ties of long standing. The years of American rule left considerable impact upon the viewpoints of the Filipino, especially in government, education, health, and sanitation. Independence strengthened these ties between the people of America and the Philippines. The Korean crisis along with the problems in Vietnam and Laos have re-emphasized the necessity for a united stand against militant aggression. The Republic must remain dependent upon United States military strength for its security in a troubled world. In turn, the Philippines must continue to provide regional leadership in Southeast Asia, not just as a showcase of democracy, but also as an economic leader among the lesser-developed countries in that part of the world. It is hoped that the Republic has had the "big push" necessary to get the economy off the launching pad, possibly into orbit. During the next twenty years we hope to see the Philippines pass through the sound barrier into sustained economic growth and mature political leadership.

Bibliography

Corpuz, O. D., *The Bureaucracy of the Philippines,* Institute of Public Administration, University of the Philippines, Manila, 1957.

Eggan, Fred, Evett D. Hester, Norton S. Ginsberg, and staff, *Area Handbook on the Philippines,* four volumes, Human Relation Area Files, Inc., New Haven, Conn., 1956.

Golay, Frank, *The Philippines: A Study in National Economic Development,* Cornell University Press, Ithaca, N. Y., 1961.

Grunder, G. A. and W. E. Livezay, *The Philippines and the United States,* University of Oklahoma Press, Norman, Okla., 1951.

Quirino, Carlos, *Magsaysay of the Philippines,* Alemars, Manila, 1958.

Ravenholt, Albert, *The Philippines: A Young Republic on the Move,* D. Van Nostrand Company, Inc., Princeton, N. J., 1962.

Romulo, Carlos P., *Crusade in Asia: Philippine Victory,* John Day Company, New York, 1955.

Spencer, J. E., *Land and People in the Philippines,* University of California Press, Berkeley and Los Angeles, 1952.

Also recommended are the relevant chapters in:

Buss, Claude A., *Southeast Asia and the World Today,* D. Van Nostrand Company, Inc., Princeton, N. J., 1958.

Butwell, Richard A., *Southeast Asia Today and Tomorrow,* Frederick A. Praeger, New York, 1961.

Cressey, George B., *Asia's Lands and Peoples,* Third edition, McGraw-Hill, New York, 1963.

Fifield, Russell F., *The Diplomacy of Southeast Asia,* 1954-1958, Harper and Row, New York, 1958.

Ginsberg, Norton, *et al., The Pattern of Asia,* Prentice Hall, Englewood Cliffs, N. J., 1958.

Kahin, George McT. (ed.), *Governments and Politics of Southeast Asia,* Cornell University Press, Ithaca, N. Y., 1959.

Spencer, J. E., *Asia, East by South,* Wiley and Sons, New York, 1954.

Thompson, W. S., *Population and Progress in the Far East,* University of Chicago Press, Chicago, 1956.

Vanderbosch, Amry, and Butwell, Richard A., *Southeast Asia Among the World Powers,* University of Kentucky Press, Lexington, 1957.

Index

Abaca, 47, 48, 56-57, 82
Aglipay, Gregorio, 41
Aglipayan religion, 41
Agrarian unrest, 10, 47
Agriculture, 46-60; acreage, 57; animal industry, 58-59; commercial, 47, 52-58; employment in, 46; evaluation of, 59-60; modernization of, 48, 53; pattern of, 47 ff.; problems, 46-47, 54; shifting cultivation, 47, 49; subsistence, 47; tenancy, 46
Aguinaldo, General Emilio, 13
Airlines, 91 (map), 92
Aluminum, processing of, 72
Americans, 25-26; at Santo Tomas, 19
Americanization, 13-18, 42 ff., 105
Animal industry, 48, 58-59
Armed forces, 97-98
Association of Southeast Asian States, 114
Australia, 65, 110, 114, 115, 121

Bacalod, 82, 89
Baguio, city, 52, 89; region, 61
Bananas, 47, 50-51
"Bases Agreement," 22, 123
Basilan, 58, 116
Bataan, 18, 37, 72
Batangas, 52, 62, 65, 75, 89; Bay, 72
Bikol region, 48
Bikolano dialect, 37
Bikolanos, 37
Birth rate, 32
Bohol, 37, 63
Borneo, 24, 117
  North Borneo, 22, 111, 118
Bukidnon plateau, 35, 50, 58
Bulacan, 52, 65
Burma, 113-114

Cagayan, plain, 35, 50; river, 49; valley, 48, 57, 58, 89
Cambodia, 112
Capital, American, 48, 72; European, 48; Filipino, 34-35, 48; for industry, 34-35, 75, 77
Catholic schools, 27, 83
Catholicism, 12, 39-40
Cavite, 52, 98
Cebu, 12, 32, 50, 53, 63, 64, 65, 70; city, 30, 81, 89, 92; province, 75
Cebuano dialect, 37
Cebuanos, 35
Cement, 70, 71-72
Central Plain, 32, 48, 80, 99
China, Nationalist, 108-109; People's Republic, 108, 109
Chinese, 11, 25; language, 38; minority, 23; schools, 38, 109; stores, 27, 30
Christianity, 8, 39-41
Chromite, 62, 63
Clark Air Force Base, 123
Coal, 64-65
Coffee, 47, 58
Coconuts, 47, 54-56
Colonial period, 10, 11-14
Commerce, coastwise, 86; interisland, 84-86; foreign, 120-121
Commonwealth, 15-18
Communist influence, 99-100, 114; party, 102
Congress, Philippine, 96; United States, 96
Constitution, 96
Copper, 62, 63-64
Corn, 47, 48, 50
Cotabato, province, 58; lowland, 39

Davao, area, 82; city, 30, 82; province, 48, 58

Economy, 10, 46, 60, 68 ff., 95, 103, 126

Education, 42-45; American influence on, 126-127; Chinese schools, 109; department of, 43, 109; enrollment, 43; importance of, 43; organization of, 29, 38, 42-45; primary, 42-43; private, 27, 43-44, 126; public, 26-27, 40, 42 ff.; secondary, 43; universities, 44-45

Emigration, 35

Employment, 55, 74-75

English language, use of, 8, 29, 38-39

Exports, 52, 54, 62, 63, 120

Farms, size of, 47

Fertilizer, manufacture of, 71

Foreign policy, 105-119, 127-128; objectives, 107

Foreign trade, 119-120

Garcia, Carlos, 23, 101, 110, 128

Gold, 61-62

Government, 96-100

Great Britain (*see* United Kingdom)

Highways, 88-90

Hiligayon, 37

Homes, 28, 30

Hong Kong, 63, 92

Hukbalahaps, 47, 99-100, 102

Hydroelectric power, 65-66

Ifugaos, 25, 48

Igorots, 11

Iligan, 35, 73, 74

Ilocos coast, 32, 57; provinces, 57

Iloilo, 30, 82

Ilokano (dialect), 37

Ilokanos, 35, 37

Ilongos, 38

Imports, 120-121

Independence, 12-13

Indonesia, 58, 114, 121; policy toward, 110-112

Interisland shipping, 84-86

Irrigation, 48-49

Iron ore, 62-63

Islam, 41

Japan, 58, 63, 64, 65; relations with, 115-117; trade with, 120, 121

Japanese occupation, 18-19

Jeepney, 90, 92

Laos, 112

Labor, agricultural, 53; manufacturing, 74-75

Laguna, 48, 65

Laguna de Bay, 49, 58

Languages, 8, 37-40

Laurel-Langley Agreement, 21, 54

Law and order, 98-100

Legaspi, city, 87

Legaspi, Miguel de, 11

Leyte, 50, 53, 57

Life, rural, 27-29; urban, 29-31

Literacy, 37

Luzon, 11, 22, 32, 48, 52, 53, 57, 62, 63, 86, 89

Macapagal, Diasdado, 23, 101-103, 105, 119

Magellan, 11, 12

Magsaysay, Ramon, 23, 100-101

Malaya, 58, 114-115

Malaysia, 118

Manila, city, 1-2, 7-8, 11, 30, 36, 44, 73-75, 80-81, 92; area, 17 (map), 36, 37, 72, 73, 98; Bay, 116; markets, 52; population, 80

Manila hemp (*see* Abaca)

Manufacturing, 68-79; growth of, 70-73; handicaps to, 76-77; home industries, 28, 69; impetus to, 75; Manila industrial District, 73-75; outlook for, 78-79; policy, 73

Manganese, 63

Maria Cristina, 65, 71, 72

Marinduque, 37, 62

Masbate, 37, 58

Mestizos, 12, 25

Mercury, 62, 64

Migration, 35-36

Mindanao, 11, 32, 35, 48, 50, 56, 63,

65, 86; settlement in, 38
Mindoro, 32, 89
Minerals, 61-67; evaluation of, 66-67; export of, 62; importance of, 61; map, 51
Missionaries, 40
Moros, 9, 11, 25, 41-42, 98-99; lawlessness, 98
Mountains, 61, 64; Sierra Madre, 106
Municipia, 12

National boundaries, 117-119
National budget, 42
National language, 39, 80
National Power Corporation, 66
National Steel and Shipbuilding Corporation, 71
Nationalism, 77, 93-96; economic nationalism, 95
Negritos, 25
Negros, 32, 53, 63, 64
Negros Occidental, 75
Nickel, 62-64

Operation Brotherhood, 113
Osmeña, Sergio, 18, 101

Palawan, 32, 63, 89
Pampanga, dialect, 37; province, 99; river, 86
Pampangans, 37
Panay, 53; plain of, 32, 48, 89
Pangasinans, 37
Petroleum, import of, 121; production, 64; refining, 72
Philippine core area, 80-81
Philippine Military Assistance Act, 21-22
Philippine Naturalization Act, 20
Philippine Rehabilitation Act, 20-21
Philippine Trade Act, 21, 53
Physiography, 8-9
Pineapples, 35, 48, 58
Plaza complex, 27
Political leadership, 102-104
Political organization, 20
Political parties: Democratic Alliance, 101; Communist, 102; Liberal, 100 ff.; *Nationalista,* 99 ff.; Progressive, 101
Population; density, 32; growth, 32-33; movement of, 35-36; problems, 33
Presidency, 96-97
Protestantism, 41
Public Law 370, 20-21
Public Law 371, 20

Quezon province, 48
Quezon, Manuel, 15, 18, 102
Quirino, Elpidio, 23, 100, 101, 110

Racial factors, 24-26
Railroads, 87-88; Manila Railroad, 65, 87, 88; Philippine Railroad, 87; private lines, 87
Ramie, 48, 52, 58
Regionalism, 9
Regional centers, 81-83
Religion, 39-42; and education, 40; and politics, 40; Catholic, 39-40; Moslem, 39, 41; Protestant, 41
Reparations, 116-117
Rice growing, 47-50
River transportation, 86-87
Romulo, Carlos, 101, 105, 111
Roxas, Manuel, 23
Rubber, 48, 58
Rural life, 27-29

Sabah (*see* Borneo)
Samar, 57, 62-64, 89
Santo Tomas, 19, 40, 44
Schools (*see* Education)
SEATO, 110-112
Shifting cultivation, 47
Southeast Asia, 7-10, 9 (map), 24; policy toward, 110-112
Spain, 57, 63, 108
Spanish, colony, 11-13; influence, 29, 40; language, 39; people, 25
Supreme Court, 96
Steel and shipyards, 70-71
Sugar, 47, 52-54, 69; export of, 82
Sulu Islands, 98; sea, 25; province, 50
Sweet potatoes, 47, 50

Tagalog, language, 37; region, 38, 80
Tagalogs, 36, 38
Taruc, Luis, 99, 100
Thailand, 113, 114
Tobacco, 47, 57-58
Transportation, 76, 83-92
Turtle Islands, 117, 118
Tydings-McDuffie Act, 15

United Nations, 70, 105-106, 108,
  111; UNESCO, 107; UNICEF, 107
United Kingdom, 61, 63, 117, 118
United States, 61, 63, 64, 111; assistance, 13, 20-22, 27, 60, 70, 71, 85,
  119; citizens, 95, 126; and the
  Philippines, 122-128; economic ties
  with, 124-126; military ties with,
  123-124; Sugar Act, 53

Urban life, 29-32
University of the Philippines, 45, 110,
  116

Vietnam, 112
Visayan dialect, 37
Visayans, 35-36
Visayas, 9, 89, 92
Vehicles, highway, 90-91

Water commerce, 84-87
Waray-Waray, 37
Westernization, 105
Women, employment of, 31, 34, 75;
  fertility of, 33-34; status of, 31-32
World War II, 7, 53, 85, 87, 99

Zambales, 63, 64
Zamboanga, 82, 83